DR. MINOTT W. LEWIS

1893–1960

A Vice President of Self-Realization Fellowship

DR. M. W. LEWIS

The Life Story of One of
the Earliest American Disciples
of Paramahansa Yogananda

SELF-REALIZATION FELLOWSHIP
Founded by Paramahansa Yogananda

Fourth edition, 1993; This printing, 2022

Authorized by the International Publications Council of
SELF-REALIZATION FELLOWSHIP

The Self-Realization Fellowship name and emblem (shown above) appear on all SRF books, recordings, and other publications, assuring the reader that a work originates with the society established by Paramahansa Yogananda and faithfully conveys his teachings

ISBN: 978-0-87612-413-0

Printed in the United States of America
1876-J6486

CONTENTS

Preface to the Fourth Edition

The year 1993, marking the centennial of Paramahansa Yogananda's birth, is also the hundredth anniversary of the birth of one of his earliest and most devout American disciples, Dr. Minott W. Lewis. In honor of Dr. Lewis's centennial, Self-Realization Fellowship is happy to publish this expanded edition of his life story.

During the many years that he served as a vice president and well-beloved minister of Self-Realization Fellowship, Doctor—as he was affectionately called by all—gave guidance in the Guru's teachings to countless Self-Realization members, who deeply valued his wise and fatherly counsel. His life of spiritual dedication continues to be a beacon of inspiration and encouragement to God-seeking souls.

Born on March 26, 1893, Dr. Lewis met the Guru in Boston in 1920, just three months after Paramahansaji's arrival in the United States. He and his wife, Mildred, and their friend Mrs. Alice Hasey, became the nucleus of the first Self-Realization meditation group in America. From the time of their first meeting, Doctor embraced the Guru's teachings with his whole heart, combining faithful practice of meditation with the responsibilities of marriage and raising two children, as well as carrying on a busy dental practice. His life demonstrated the power of Yoga to elevate the sincere and dedicated disciple to great heights of spiritual awareness.

For this new edition, an essay by Dr. Lewis and three lectures given by him at Self-Realization Fellowship temples have been added, providing additional anecdotes about his long and inspiring association with Paramahansa Yogananda. Also added is the text of the eulogy delivered at the memorial service for Mildred Lewis, who passed on at the age of 90 in 1988.

SELF-REALIZATION FELLOWSHIP

September 1993
Los Angeles, California

DR. M. W. LEWIS

The Life Story of Dr. M. W. Lewis

Paramahansaji's Faithful Disciple for Forty Years

"As We Started, So Let Us Finish"

Forty years of faithful discipleship under a great master were climaxed by a glorious upliftment at death for Dr. Minott White Lewis, a beloved vice president of Self-Realization Fellowship.

After a brief illness in March, Dr. Lewis entered Scripps Memorial Hospital in La Jolla, California, on April 7, 1960.

On the evening of April 13, following a short nap, Doctor sat up to meditate—a practice he followed religiously every night and morning. At Doctor's bedside was his loyal wife and fellow disciple on the path, Mildred Lewis. Sitting in silence, Doctor entered Infinity in a manner awe-inspiring. Mildred was blessed by perceiving the presence of Sri Yukteswar (the guru of Paramahansaji).*

An Early Experience: A Divine Voice Speaks

Dr. Lewis was born on March 26, 1893, in Somerville, Massachusetts, the son of Stephen H. Lewis, a building contractor, and Laura Wright Lewis. Minott had two sisters, Grace and Laura; and one brother—the late Wilbur F. Lewis, president of Winter Hill Savings and Loan Bank of Somerville, who also served two terms in the Massachusetts Legislature. The Lewis family attended the Methodist Episcopal Church.

Doctor sometimes related the following childhood experience:

"When I was quite young I had a mischievous nature and caused lots of trouble to my brother and sisters, especially the latter. I was having a grand time one day and the situation got out of hand. My mother, a woman of highly developed spiritual nature, was in her room at the end of a long hall. I was at the other end of the hall. In the midst of the teasing episode a voice came out of the ether, saying: 'Minie,† stop teasing your sisters—be a good boy and go downstairs!'

*Further information is given in article on pages 53–54.

†Minott was called "Minie," a nickname, by his family.

This photograph of Dr. Lewis was taken in November 1948 while he was on a one-week visit to Phoenix with Paramahansa Yogananda.

"That voice was heard clearly not only by me but by two others: the maid on the lower floor and my mother in her room at the end of the upstairs hall. When I called down to the maid: 'Did you hear that voice, Margaret?' She said that she had. My mother, speaking from her distant room, also said: 'I heard the voice.'

"Some thirty years later Paramahansa Yogananda walked through that upper hall and saw a spiritual light flash at the exact spot where the divine voice had spoken to me so many years before."

Graduation From College and Entry Into Dental Practice

Minott graduated from high school in West Somerville in 1911, and enrolled in the Dentistry School of Tufts College (later Tufts University) in Boston. He received his D.M.D. (Doctor of Dental Medicine) degree in 1914, and entered dental practice. During 1915 and 1916 Dr. Lewis also served as an instructor of clinical dentistry at Tufts College.

In 1916 Dr. Lewis married Mildred M. Wentworth of Dover, New Hampshire. Her family were members of the Congregationalist Church. In addition to Mrs. Lewis's long and selfless cooperation with Doctor in spreading the Self-Realization message, she engaged in many civic activities. During the Second World War years she served as a volunteer worker in Boston at the Children's Hospital and with the Red Cross Motor Corps.

The Lewises had two children: J. Bradford Lewis, retired vice president of Belz Industries, Mineola, New York; and Brenda (Mrs. John Rosser). Mr. and Mrs. Rosser contributed much time to Self-Realization lay disciple activities in San Diego, California.

"You Should Meet Swami Yogananda"

Dr. Lewis's wife, Mildred, met Paramahansa Yogananda before Doctor did. Paramahansaji arrived in America in September 1920. He had been invited to Boston by the American Unitarian Association as the Indian delegate to an International Congress of Religious Liberals. After addressing the congress on October 6, he accepted numerous invitations to speak before churches and philosophical groups.

It was during this period that Mrs. Lewis attended a lecture given by a leader of the Rosicrucian Order, and was invited to remain after the meeting so that the leader could introduce her to "a gentleman from India." Thus Mildred met Swami Yogananda, as he was then known. A few pleasantries were exchanged; and Mrs. Lewis returned home, eager to tell Doctor about the Hindu with long black hair curling over his shoulders, wearing an orange robe and a turban. Dr. Lewis asked her many questions. A few days later he hurried home from his office to tell Mrs. Lewis that he had passed by the swami on the street. Many people in town were eager to know more about this mysterious person from India.

Meanwhile, Mrs. Alice Hasey (later Sister Yogmata), a longtime friend of Dr. Lewis, had met Paramahansa Yogananda at the West Somerville Unitarian Church, where he had been a guest of the pastor. She invited Paramahansaji to her home to meet a group of friends who were interested in metaphysics. Soon after, Mrs. Hasey talked with Dr. Lewis. "You should meet Swami Yogananda," she said.

An appointment was made for Christmas Eve at Unity House, where the Master had a room. When Doctor left his home to keep this engagement he thought he would be gone just a short time. He told

Paramahansa Yogananda *(center)* with Self-Realization students, Chelsea, Massachusetts, 1921. Mrs. Lewis and Doctor are first and second from left. The second woman from right is Mrs. Alice Hasey (Sister Yogmata), who fulfilled Sri Yukteswar's "strawberry prophecy" (*Autobiography of a Yogi,* Chapter 21). This is probably the first picture taken in America of a group of Self-Realization students.

Mildred that he would be back soon to decorate the Christmas tree.

On his way to Unity House, Doctor recalled parental warnings against being deceived or misled by charlatans who pose as religious teachers; his frame of mind was skeptical.

Paramahansaji received Dr. Lewis warmly. Placing a tigerskin on the floor, the Guru asked Doctor to sit cross-legged on it, and then sat down opposite him. The young dentist had many spiritual questions on his mind, and Paramahansaji gave him satisfying answers.

Many years later, Doctor said of this occasion, "I was 'from Missouri,' and I had to be shown. Worse than that, I was from New England, and I had to *know*!"

On that Christmas Eve in 1920 he said to Paramahansaji:

"The Bible tells us: 'The light of the body is the eye: if therefore thine eye be single, thy whole body shall be full of light.'* Can you explain this?"

"I think so," the Guru replied.

Doctor was still doubtful. "I have asked many persons," he said, "but no one seems to know the meaning."

"Can the blind lead the blind?" Paramahansaji responded. "Both would fall into the same ditch of error."

"Can *you* show me these things?"

"I think so," the Master reiterated.

"Then, for Heaven's sake, please show me!"

A Transforming Experience on Christmas Eve

Paramahansaji then showed Doctor the light of the spiritual eye and of the thousand-petaled lotus in the brain.† Looking directly into Doctor's eyes, Paramahansaji asked:

"Will you always love me as I love you?"

Doctor replied in the affirmative.

Then the Guru said, "Your sins are forgiven and I take charge of your life." He added, "I want you to promise that you will never avoid me." Doctor promised.

Of this pact between guru and disciple Doctor said later, "Many times it was very difficult, for the discipline of a guru is not easy; but it is always for your highest good, guiding you to the abode of Light."

* Matthew 6:22.

† Yoga treatises explain that there are seven subtle centers of life and consciousness in man's spine and brain that radiate rays of life-giving light and energy.

Minott W. Lewis at age eighteen, when he graduated from high school in West Somerville, Massachusetts, in 1911

Dr. and Mrs. Lewis at Encinitas Hermitage, where they hosted Mexican and South American Self-Realizationists, August 1957

After showing Dr. Lewis how to see the light of the spiritual eye, and giving him other spiritual instruction, Paramahansaji asked him if he thought other Americans would be interested in these teachings.

"Yes, I do," Doctor replied.

"Then," the Guru said, "after you practice what I have taught you, if these techniques of meditation appeal to you and benefit you, will you help others to know about them?"

"I certainly will," said Doctor.

"I Knew Some Great Good Would Come From Paramahansa Yogananda"

Telling of this incident many years later, at the dedication of the Self-Realization Ashram Center in Encinitas, Doctor said:

"That is why, friends, I have been interested in Self-Realization Fellowship, and that is why I have tried to help; because I knew that some good, some great good, would come from Paramahansa Yogananda. America has given me much, and I am thankful for it; but there is one thing that America did not give me, and that is the spiritual realization and understanding I received from India; they came to me from Paramahansa Yogananda."

It was two o'clock on that Christmas morning in 1920 when Doctor returned home from his appointment with the Guru. Mrs. Lewis had been understandably alarmed by his long absence; but when she saw his face, she realized that the meeting of her husband with Paramahansaji had been a transforming experience.

Doctor had promised to decorate the family Christmas tree; instead, his Guru had illuminated for him the inner spinal Christmas tree. Often afterward, when telling of this divine awakening, Doctor said, "It was my first real Christmas!"

A Meditation Group Started in Boston

With the help of Doctor and Sister Yogmata, Paramahansaji started a meditation group of Yogoda students.* He gave many lectures. But, as he wryly related in later years, "Just a few people would come. Sister

*The word *Yogoda* is the name by which Paramahansa Yogananda's work in India is known: Yogoda Satsanga Society of India. He also used this term in America in the early years. "Yogoda," a word coined by Paramahansaji, is derived from *yoga,* union, harmony, equilibrium; and *da,* that which imparts. *Satsanga* means "divine fellowship," or "fellowship with Truth." For the West, he translated the Indian name as "Self-Realization Fellowship."

RAJARSI JANAKANANDA AND DR. M. W. LEWIS

Rajarsi Janakananda (James J. Lynn), second president of Self-Realization Fellowship, and Dr. M. W. Lewis, vice president, outside the Hermitage, Encinitas, 1952. Like Rajarsi, Dr. Lewis greatly helped Self-Realization Fellowship by generous donations.

In a speech in Encinitas on January 8, 1938, Paramahansa Yogananda said: "Men can carry on successfully in business life and yet find time to meditate and think of God. Mr. Lynn and Dr. Lewis have developed greatly in the spiritual path, while performing their worldly duties."

and I used to sit and talk about how this teaching would spread all over the country. 'Many big places will materialize!' I would say. Dr. Lewis would exclaim, 'But when?'"

Doctor and Sister Yogmata gave generously whenever help was needed. In addition to sponsoring his lectures, they also gave financial aid when Paramahansaji undertook the building of a little hermitage at Hardy's Pond, near Waltham, Massachusetts, in 1922. Here the Boston group of Yogoda students enjoyed many happy hours of meditation with the Guru.

Doctor told brother disciples of an incident when he came to know in a divine way of Paramahansaji's need for financial assistance:

"I had started one day from my home, where Swamiji was staying at the time, and had not gone far when suddenly I felt I must go back and give him some financial aid. This was just as clear to me as if an audible voice had said, 'Turn around and go back and help.' I felt through intuition that Lahiri Mahasaya* and Sri Yukteswarji were both asking me to do something; and so strong was the feeling, I turned right around, went back, and gave him the assistance he required. When I did, his eyes filled with tears, because he knew that God had responded to his needs, and that the Divine Voice had silently spoken to me."

Paramahansaji Demonstrates His Loving Omnipresence

The following story illustrates how a true guru, through his omnipresent divine consciousness, is aware of every need of his disciple and is able to render instant aid:

One Sunday in July 1921, Doctor and Mrs. Lewis drove with their children to the summer home of Dr. Lewis's parents in South Duxbury, Massachusetts. It was a very warm, humid day. Early in the afternoon dark clouds began to gather.

Nevertheless, Doctor, his father, and his brother decided to go for a sail. Their skiff was rather light, but they confidently set off from shore in a brisk breeze. When they were about two miles out, the cloudiness in the sky deepened. An ominous calm settled over the sea.

Doctor and his brother lowered the sail and started to row for shore. They were not able to row for long, however, because a great wind

*Lahiri Mahasaya (guru of Swami Sri Yukteswar) is one of the line of Gurus of Self-Realization Fellowship (Yogoda Satsanga Society of India). His life is described in Paramahansaji's *Autobiography of a Yogi.*

Dr. Lewis making gesture of *pranam,* the traditional Indian obeisance, before pictures of Lahiri Mahasaya, Mahavatar Babaji, Jesus Christ, Swami Sri Yukteswar, and Paramahansa Yogananda during closing benediction at 1957 Convocation garden party, Self-Realization Fellowship Lake Shrine, Pacific Palisades, California

started up, tossing the boat around like a chip of wood. Hail pelted down. The two brothers immediately led their father into the cockpit of the boat; it took all their strength to pull the canvas cover over him and to crawl under it themselves. Soon the sea was a boiling mass of foam; lightning flashed, and thunder boomed around them.

"When in Trouble, Look in the *Aum*"

"I remember thinking, 'This is the end,'" Doctor related afterward, "and I wondered what it would be like. Then I thought of my wife and two little children, and I thought of Yoganandaji—of how I had just started with him, and things had seemed so bright; and now they were to be cut off. I remember feeling in my heart a deep desire for his help, and then his words came to me. He had once said, 'Remember, Doctor, if ever you are in trouble, look in the *Aum* (the vibratory light of God, which can be seen inwardly at the point between the eyebrows). If you look there and see His light and feel His presence, no harm can come.'

The Light of God Dissolves the Danger

"I looked through the spiritual eye in the forehead, and that light

Mrs. Mildred Lewis, Doctor, and Paramahansa Yogananda on picnic celebrating Doctor's birthday; in Cleveland National Forest near Palomar Mountain, California, March 26, 1946

came—a great light—as I lay there in the bottom of the boat. And with its radiance came such an assurance, I didn't care what happened; because I knew nothing could touch me. I knew that God had responded through my Guru."

The storm abated and the three men looked out from under the canvas covering, scanning the shore in the hope that someone would come for them. At last they spied a boat headed in their direction. They were soon towed ashore — exhausted but safe. Their families, who had been waiting for them on the beach, cried with joy to see them alive.

"Late in the afternoon we started home," Doctor recounted, "and arrived there about eleven o'clock that night. Just as I came in the door the telephone rang. Swamiji's voice said to me, 'Aha, Doctor! you came near getting wet, didn't you?'

"Well, delusion is pretty strong, and I replied casually. But again he said, 'You came near getting wet.'

"Then I answered, 'Yes, how did you know?'

"He wouldn't say anything more; but some time later, when I was talking with Sister Yogmata about this episode, she told me that Master had been at her home in West Somerville on the afternoon of the storm. He was reading a passage about the sea by Emerson. Suddenly he threw the book down and began pacing back and forth.

" 'Sister,' he said, 'Doctor is in trouble. He is in real trouble.'

"This happened at precisely the hour at which we were caught in the storm at sea.

"I told Master about what Sister Yogmata had said. 'Is it so, sir?' I asked. Swamiji just quietly dropped his head and smiled a little and nodded, 'Yes.' "

Close Calculations of Time and Tide

There were other adventures. In April 1921 Dr. and Mrs. Lewis drove Paramahansaji and a small party of students to a little island resort off the coast of Massachusetts. The plan was to stay there for a week. On the first day the weather was very cold, and sleet was falling. The temperature remained cool, although the weather did improve, and on some days there was sunshine. On one such day the Guru asked Doctor to go for a walk on the beach to a breakwater that ran out some distance into the bay. When they reached their destination, the tide was far out; the high rocks were dry.

"Let us meditate here," Paramahansaji said. They seated themselves cross-legged on the rocks, and Dr. Lewis thought it would be wonderful to meditate there in the sunshine.

The Master was soon deep within, but Doctor was battling the forces without. The rocks were hard, the sun bright, the air brisk. He saw the great calmness of Paramahansaji, and thought, "If Master can do it, I can do it." Time sped on, and after tremendous effort ("probably on Guruji's part as well as mine," Doctor said), the disciple felt great tranquility. More time passed, and occasionally Doctor would look carefully about to see how close the tidewater was coming. Watching its inevitable approach, Doctor frequently affirmed: "If he can stay, I can stay."

A Secret Blessing From the Trial on the Rocks

Five hours passed. The Master opened his eyes just as a great wave was about to splash over them. "Doctor, Doctor!" Paramahansaji exclaimed. "Let's get out of here!" Guru and disciple departed with speed. Later Doctor said, "That test of sitting with Master for five hours on the rocks while the tide was rising removed from me forever all feelings of restlessness during long periods of meditation."

Paramahansaji continued to spread his message in Boston. Among the first students in his Yogoda classes were Dr. and Mrs. Lewis, Sister Yogmata, Doctor's sister Laura W. Elliott, Raymond Elliott, George Carpenter, Mr. Au Claire, Mrs. Alta Walker, Miss May Murray, and Mr. Amos Jones, all of West Somerville; Mr. Gerard, his mother, Mr. Beck, Dr. Perrin, professor at Boston University, and Mrs. Jessie Southwick, head of the Emerson School of Oratory, all of Boston; and Mrs. Sargent of the Sargent School of Physical Education in Cambridge.

Dr. Lewis assumed the leadership of the Boston Center when the Guru went to New York City in late 1923. Paramahansaji's first lecture in New York, at Town Hall, aroused immense interest. He accepted an invitation from the management of the Hotel Pennsylvania in New York to be its guest.

During the years that Doctor conducted the Boston Center it was necessary for him to drive from his home in Arlington, Massachusetts, to Boston. Often he would be pressed for time.

A Divine Force Saves Lives of Doctor and Two Other Students

On one evening his sister, Mrs. Laura Elliott, and Sister Yogmata were with him. It was a winter night, and the road was covered with ice

Dr. M. W. Lewis, vice president of Self-Realization Fellowship; and Sri Daya Mata, president, at Encinitas Hermitage, April 1955

(From left) Sister Yogmata, one of the first Self-Realization students in America; Paramahansa Yogananda; Dr. and Mrs. Lewis; at SRF International Headquarters in Los Angeles, December 26, 1944. In a talk after the dinner, Paramahansaji reminisced about the joys and hard times of his early years in America, and expressed appreciation for the loving support of Sister Yogmata and the Lewises. He said, "I have happy memories of the days when Doctor and Sister and I used to talk over the future of the organization....The dreams I have had, and have worked for, God has fulfilled."

and snow. They approached a narrow bridge on a slight rise in the roadway. Traveling rather fast as they reached the level of the bridge, they saw before them a car that had skidded sideways on the ice, blocking their way. The bridge was so narrow, there was no room to pass on either side of the disabled car. A crash seemed inevitable. The thought flashed through Doctor's mind: "Why should this happen? We are going to our Yogoda meeting."

At that instant a great force seemed to take hold of the car, stopping it before it reached the obstructing vehicle. Doctor said it was as if a giant had reached down his hand and held back the automobile.

Sister Yogmata and Mrs. Elliott were momentarily speechless; they knew that in that moment they had been protected by God. Sister

Yogmata spoke first. "Doctor, did you feel that great force?"

"I did, Sister," Dr. Lewis replied. "We could never have stopped otherwise."

Boston Students Welcome the Guru on His Return in 1928

In 1924 Paramahansaji left New York on a cross-country trip. In 1925 he acquired Mount Washington Estates in Los Angeles and made it the headquarters of Self-Realization Fellowship.* He continued his speaking tours, and made a triumphal return to Boston in 1928. When he arrived on September 19 he was welcomed by Governor Alvan Fuller at the State House. A capacity audience of 2500 greeted him enthusiastically at his opening lecture in Symphony Hall. On the welcoming committee with Dr. and Mrs. Lewis were many prominent Bostonians; noted musicians entertained. In addition to giving two weeks of classes, Paramahansaji gave lectures at a score of Boston clubs and philanthropic organizations, and spoke over radio stations WNAC, WBZ, and WLOE. On November 11 he addressed students at Harvard University. An account in *East-West* magazine (now *Self-Realization*) states that his lecture at Harvard Union Club "was received with deafening applause and sustained cheering."

The Guru and Doctor Meet in Chicago at World's Fair

In 1933 Paramahansa Yogananda was invited to speak before the

*In 1935, the Mt. Washington center was established as the international headquarters, the Mother Center, of Paramahansa Yogananda's work worldwide.

Paramahansa Yogananda *(circled)*, Dr. Lewis *(to the right of Paramahansaji)*, and members of a Yogoda (Self-Realization) class held in Unity House, Boston, 1928

World Fellowship of Faiths at the Chicago World's Fair. He took with him a small party of disciples from the SRF Mt. Washington Center. Doctor Lewis traveled from Boston to Chicago to be with his Guru on this important occasion. Here Doctor met for the first time Miss Faye Wright, Paramahansaji's disciple since 1931, later Sri Daya Mata, president of Self-Realization Fellowship.

In 1935 Sri Yogananda left for India, at the behest of his guru Swami Sri Yukteswarji. That year Sri Yukteswar conferred upon him the title of *Paramahansa,* the highest spiritual title in India.

The Master returned to the United States late in 1936, and on January 3, 1937, a Self-Realization Convocation Banquet was held at the international headquarters in Los Angeles. Dr. Lewis attended the festive affair and gave a brief address. He said:

"I am very happy to be here with Swamiji, and to bring to you the greetings of Boston. Words cannot express my feeling. I shall have to let my heart speak its own language. In wishing you all the happiest of new years in 1937, I think the greatest wish I can give you is that you will have deep spiritual realization and that you will find God in your meditation. Dive deep in the ocean of Spirit, and if you don't find Him at the first dive, plunge deeper. As Swamiji says, find fault with your diving. I might add a humble suggestion: When you dive, mentally take Swamiji's hand. He knows where the pearls of wisdom are. He knows the Spirit. He can show you God."

The Boston Center continued to thrive. Weekly meetings were held in the homes of two different Self-Realization students. On March 1, 1937, the Boston group had as guest speaker Dr. A. K. Mukherji of India, a disciple of Bhupendra Sanyal Mahasaya (an eminent disciple of Lahiri Mahasaya).

Boston Center Holds Annual Yogoda Festival

In June of the same year the Boston group held its annual Yogoda Festival—a traditional Indian ceremony initiated by Paramahansaji at the home of Sister Yogmata in 1920 and carried on loyally by the Boston Self-Realization students. The secretary wrote the following report to the SRF Mother Center:

"As each laid his tribute of a flower upon the altar, kneeling to breathe a prayer, the room *was* Light and *Aum* was upon and through each....Dr. Lewis was divinely inspired—in his prayers, in the vibration of his tone—moving us to recognition of the Master's holy presence."

Paramahansa Yogananda and Dr. Lewis at the World's Fair in Chicago, October 1933, where the Master addressed a meeting of the World's Fellowship of Faiths on "The Art of Living"

The Divine Relationship Between Master and Disciple

Dr. Lewis traveled to Los Angeles to be present for the Second Convocation of Self-Realization teachers and students, held in December 1937. When he was called upon to speak, Dr. Lewis's words were drawn from a well of love for Paramahansaji. He said:

"I chose the subject, 'My Guru,' because that theme is nearest and dearest to me. All spiritual realization that I have or hope to have I owe to him, my guru, Paramahansa Yogananda. When I first sat at his feet, back in 1920, my heart was filled with honest doubt. But when he taught me and I saw the compassion in his eyes, I was overwhelmed. Something sprang up within me that had been sleeping, something that I had forgotten; and it has been present with me ever since. Ordinary human ties and friendships pale in the light of that divine relationship between master and disciple.

"Many times I came to Paramahansaji with my troubles, but I could not disturb his calmness. I remember that I said to him on one of these occasions, 'How is it you are able to have such courage and conviction?' He replied, 'Doctor, remember: the same Father who protects me, protects you. He is our common Father.' That thought has been a source of inspiration as I have plodded along the path."

In an article that appeared in the April 1937 issue of *Inner Culture* (now *Self-Realization*), Doctor Lewis wrote the following about his Guru:

"As we sat together on the tigerskin rug enjoying God's presence, and I looked into his face, I saw no show of consciousness of superior ability. He might well have expressed it; for to be able, by such great calmness and realization, to help another to feel the Divine Consciousness is no mean accomplishment. But instead there was present an expression of humbleness, love, and supreme satisfaction that another of God's children was able, like himself, to enjoy the presence and bliss of the Lord, our common Father. Such humility has been and always will be a deep inspiration to me. To my mind, it is a characteristic of true greatness."

(Upper right) Dr. and Mrs. Lewis *(garlanded)* and their daughter Brenda *(wearing pearl necklace)*. The Encinitas Ashram Center residents shown here had lovingly arranged this India-style welcome for Dr. and Mrs. Lewis upon their return to Encinitas from a trip to Boston, November 27, 1956.

Dr. and Mrs. M. W. Lewis with Paramahansa Yogananda, outside Self-Realization Fellowship Hermitage, Encinitas, California, 1939.

Dr. and Mrs. Lewis Make Yearly Cross-Country Trips

The Lewises became regular cross-country travelers, making two trips from Boston every year—one in the summer and one in the Christmas-holiday period.

On January 2, 1938, Dr. Lewis was present in Encinitas, California, for the formal opening of the SRF Golden Lotus Temple. Paramahansaji had to conduct two services, as there was not even standing room for the hundreds that assembled for the first scheduled ceremony. In all, 3,000 persons attended the dedication.

In 1941 Mrs. Elizabeth Backus of La Jolla, California, the Lewises, and several other devoted students donated to the SRF Mother Center a fine Robert Morton pipe organ. It was played for the first time at a banquet in July by the noted organist, Mr. Karl Krebs of Santa Barbara, California.

Paramahansaji Praises the Work of Dr. Lewis at Boston Center

Late in 1941 Paramahansaji visited the Boston Center again. He wrote the following account of his visit for the April 1942 issue of *Inner Culture:*

"It was a great pleasure to me to see the wonderful work carried on by Dr. M. W. Lewis in Boston.

"My wish to stay in a pleasant Boston apartment was fulfilled, thanks to Dr. and Mrs. Lewis. I had a delightful time. After I came to Boston in 1920, I lived in a single room without bath, and that is why I had a desire to stay in a modern apartment in Boston.

"I am grateful also for the handsome gift of a new Dodge car through the kindness of Dr. and Mrs. Lewis, Mr. and Mrs. Roscoe Elliott (Mrs. Elliott is Doctor's sister), and a few Philadelphia students. A great need for another car at the Mt. Washington Center in Los Angeles has thus been fulfilled."

Doctor and Paramahansaji Bereft of Their Fathers in 1942

Guruji's father died in July 1942, and in the same year Doctor's father passed away. Paramahansaji, in keeping with Hindu custom, composed a poem in honor of "Grandpa Lewis," which appeared in the October 1942 issue of *Inner Culture.* It read, in part:

We grieve for our losing you,
But gladden for your freedom true
From old age's limitations
And fleshly lamentations.
Your children's love,
And your most spiritual son, Minott's,
    meditation treasure
Saved in vault of karma above,
Have helped you beyond measure....

I searched your soul and name...
And I was glad to see
You basking in His grace
For your heart's quality.

Some years ago, while walking on the beach at San Clemente with the Guru and several disciples, Doctor said to Paramahansaji: "Here we are all so happy together, and then someday we shall have to part."

Paramahansaji replied: "What do you mean? We'll know each other better on the other side."

One by One, the "Big Places" Foretold Are Materialized

On Sunday, August 30, 1942, Dr. Lewis was again in Los Angeles, to

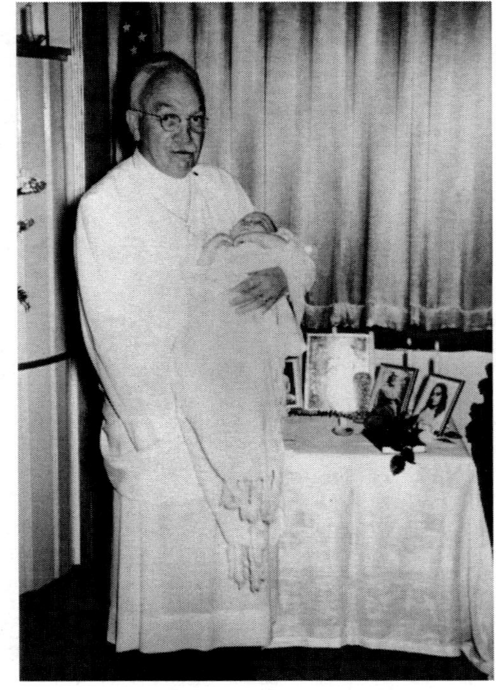

Dr. Lewis holding David Sayer, whom he christened on April 18, 1954, at the Self-Realization Temple, San Diego

Mrs. Lewis, Brother Bhaktananda, and Doctor on grounds of the SRF ashram at Encinitas, California, during 1953 Convocation

attend the dedication services at a new Self-Realization temple in Hollywood. Dr. and Mrs. Lewis had helped most generously in the acquisition of the site. At the dedication ceremonies Doctor played on the new pipe organ the ancient Sanskrit temple song, *Brahmanandam* or "Hymn to Spirit." His rendition of this beautiful melody was a favorite with Self-Realizationists through the years. Paramahansaji often asked him to play it at services.

Dr. Lewis was a guest speaker at the dedication of a new SRF temple in San Diego, California, on September 5, 1943. In discussing the effect that the teachings had had on his life, Dr. Lewis said: "I think Paramahansaji's most potent weapon is the example of his wonderful character. Today he is dedicating a temple. I want to say that twenty-three years ago he also dedicated to God another kind of temple—a shrine within my soul. The light of that temple has been with me ever since and has been my deepest inspiration."

Sister Yogmata, Dr. and Mrs. Lewis Honored at Banquet

Guruji often said: "I counsel the path of renunciation for those who wish to make a serious search for God; but to those who are already married I say, 'Follow the example of Lahiri Mahasaya.'" Doctor sought to pattern his life after that of Lahiri Mahasaya, the ideal householder-yogi.

A gala banquet was held at the Mother Center on December 26, 1944, in honor of Sister Yogmata and Dr. and Mrs. Lewis. Reminiscing about the old days, Guruji spoke of the hard times they had had and of how Sister and Dr. Lewis had helped. He said, "I have happy memories of the days when Doctor and Sister and I used to talk over the future of the organization. All those ideas have materialized. I am very glad that Doctor and Mildred have been with me many times since, to enjoy God's bounties with me. I knew that some day Sister Yogmata would visit here, too. The Lord never tells me anything that does not come true.

"So I am very happy that Sister is here, and that the things we had planned and have worked for, God has given to us—and much more than we had planned. It is only because Mt. Washington Center has always striven to be an instrument of God that those plans have been realized.

"I never forgot you, Sister, and the parts you and Dr. and Mrs. Lewis have played in my life. I want you to know that. It is a great joy to me that you are here with us today.

"So I am very much pleased that we started a center in Boston, and pleased with this gathering of souls here today. It is the culmination of so many materialized thoughts, and we are all very happy. Let us give a cheer for Sister, Doctor, and Mrs. Lewis!"

Dr. and Mrs. Lewis, Residents of Ashram Center in Encinitas

In September 1945 Dr. and Mrs. Lewis left Boston for California to reside at the SRF Encinitas Ashram Center. Later Doctor said:

"I left Boston and my profession of thirty-five years, on what my patients thought was an extended leave of absence. Many of them continued to write me asking when I was coming back. I began to feel uncertain of my course. 'Should I remain permanently in Encinitas?' I asked Master. 'Yes,' he replied, 'the Lord wants it. You are performing a greater work in Encinitas.' From that moment I knew everything was all right; I felt no further restlessness. God had spoken to me through the Guru."

In addition to his spiritual duties in Encinitas, in 1946 Dr. Lewis took over the supervision of activities at the papaya grove then being operated by Self-Realization Fellowship.

In 1946 Dr. Lewis was made a member of the Board of Directors of Self-Realization Fellowship. In that year he also became third vice president. (In 1952 Dr. Lewis was elected first vice president, and held that office until his death.)

"Dr. and Mrs. Lewis Have Led Exemplary Lives"

The members from San Diego and Encinitas regularly attended the Thursday evening services Dr. Lewis conducted at the Encinitas Hermitage. Guruji, as always, was appreciative. Speaking before a great throng at the formal dedication of the Golden Lotus Towers on the border of the ashram center site in Encinitas on February 20, 1948, Paramahansaji said:

"On Thursday nights you should come to meditate in the Hermitage with Dr. Lewis, who is a very wonderful, spiritual man. In his company you will feel great happiness....He and his wife, during the twenty-eight years that I have known them, have led exemplary lives. Doctor's presence itself will be of great help to you. Dr. and Mrs. Lewis were among my first friends in Boston. Those who have been our friends in need we remember always.

"I have never forgotten those early days. Dr. Lewis has steadfastly followed this path with great zeal. So be sure to come on Thursday nights to hear him. He gives not only words but the Spirit behind the words."

Two days later, on February 22, Paramahansaji presided at the dedication of yet another "big place"—the new chapel in Long Beach.* Dr. and Mrs. Lewis generously helped in the purchase of this handsome Normandy-style property overlooking the Pacific Ocean.

Seven hundred guests assembled at a garden party held on July 31, 1949, in Beverly Hills in honor of Paramahansa Yogananda. Dr. Lewis and other speakers told of their experiences with the Master.

"I met Paramahansa Yogananda nearly thirty years ago," Doctor said. "At that time he asked me if I thought Americans would be receptive to these teachings. 'Yes,' I replied, 'because there are many people like me, who are searching and searching for God, yet cannot find Him.'

"Paramahansaji has given us a practical way to know God and the eternal truths. If we merely talk and theorize about Him, what good is it? If we know God through personal experience, though, it is the greatest thing in life."

The Lewises made an enjoyable three-week visit to Boston in October 1949, during which time Doctor conducted three meetings of the Boston Center.†

In the spring of 1950 Dr. Lewis began conducting Sunday services at the Self-Realization Fellowship Temple in San Diego, alternating with Dr. Lloyd Kennell.‡ In his years as a Self-Realization Fellowship minister, he often shared with his audiences uplifting stories about Paramahansaji. Drawing on his personal experiences, he was able to bring light and life to his talks on the value of the Guru's teachings, and to illustrate the bond of unconditional love and friendship that exists between the guru and every sincere disciple.

"Just Like a Mother"

During a Sunday lecture on "The Mother Aspect of God," Doctor said, "The guru supports the disciple. He may be stern—the Master used to be terrifically stern with me—but when I needed his help, he

* The Long Beach Chapel was outgrown by 1967, in which year the congregation moved to a more spacious Self-Realization Temple in Fullerton, California.

† Doctor's son, J. Bradford Lewis, conducted the meetings at the Boston Center from 1949 to 1954, when he left Boston to live near Mineola, New York.

‡ Lloyd Kennell, M.D., met Paramahansa Yogananda in 1933. From 1943, when the SRF San Diego Temple was founded, until 1956, Dr. Kennell regularly conducted inspiring services at this temple. He passed away in 1957.

Dr. Lewis and Self-Realization Fellowship President Sri Daya Mata, at a reception on June 27, 1955, SRF India Hall, Los Angeles

always gave it to me. He didn't coddle me. The guru gives strength and support, not coddling."

Doctor then told of a time at Mt. Washington when he was to assist the Master in leading the All-Day Christmas Meditation, a tradition started by Paramahansaji in which one whole day is set aside for deep meditation and communion with Christ. The night before, Dr. Lewis had been stricken with a serious back problem, which left him unable to move and in a great deal of pain.

Having made the trip to the Mother Center especially to take part in this meditation, which is one of the spiritual highlights of the year for Self-Realization members, Doctor now felt there was no way he would be able to sit through the long meditation. He describes Paramahansaji's loving concern:

"All through the night before the meditation, when I was suffering, the Master kept coming to my room, bringing either an electric heating pad to put on my back or something else to ease the pain, and trying to get it back in place. He was just like a mother—no, better than a mother."

In the morning when Paramahansaji came to see how Doctor was faring, he found the disciple still immobilized with pain. Doctor told him he had done his best to overcome the condition, but that there was no way he could participate in the meditation.

"You must attend," the Master replied. "Get up." Quietly but insistently he encouraged Doctor to rise—to resist the thought of physical limitations imposed by body-consciousness.

"I can't even move enough to dress myself," Doctor protested. Again the Guru gently insisted that he try. He helped Doctor to get out of bed and assisted him in dressing himself. In his pain, Dr. Lewis was convinced he could not get down the stairs to the chapel on the main floor of the Mother Center. But with his Guru's help, he said, "somehow I got there. And for seven hours I sat there in meditation."

During that meditation, Doctor later confided, he was blessed with tremendous spiritual realizations. The great spiritual eye of divine perception was revealed to him, and his consciousness entered the light and beauty of the subtle astral realms.*

"If the Master had coddled me rather than supporting and encouraging me," he concluded, "I would not have received the great blessing that came that day. By his insistence, for which I can never repay him, Master gave me this wonderful demonstration of what is waiting for each of us on the other side of this earthly life. If you can get into the light of God, no pain or anything else can touch you. That is what Master showed me. In that consciousness there is nothing to be afraid of, nothing to worry about. There is nothing but peace and joy and security. Each of us has to be able to enter that light consciously. Regular meditation and devotion, following the path of Self-Realization, will bring you to that blessed state."

Doctor Experiences His Guru's Healing Power

In another sermon, "Can Thought Change Matter?" Dr. Lewis said:

"The following personal experience shows that a strong mind can

* Behind the physical world of matter, Yoga teaches, there exists a subtle astral world of light and energy, and a causal or ideational world of thought. Every being, every object, every vibration on the physical plane has an astral counterpart, for in the astral universe (heaven) is the "blueprint" of the material universe.

"Everything beautiful in this world is but a gross copy of the radiant grandeur of the astral world," Paramahansaji said. "Nothing material can compare with those wondrous visions of the inner world. Spiritual consciousness brings astral perception of the wisdom and beauty that is behind all material phenomena."

PARAMAHANSAJI AND THREE BELOVED DISCIPLES

Rajarsi Janakananda (J. J. Lynn), Paramahansaji, Yogacharya J. Oliver Black, and Dr. Lewis; Self-Realization Fellowship International Headquarters, Los Angeles, California, Christmas Day, 1946

prevent even the formation in another person's mind of a pattern that would cause an undesirable change in matter: One day several years ago Paramahansaji and I had just arrived at Mt. Washington Center in his automobile. He left the car and went on ahead. As I was getting out, the car door was accidently shut on three of my fingers, up to the second joints. The fingers were flattened to the actual shape of the doorjamb; the physical pain was excruciating. There was also great mental pain; for I was sure the accident meant hospitalization, which would prevent my returning next day to Boston as planned.

"The Master, who was by this time inside the building, was immediately informed of my mishap. From that instant a wall seemed to be placed between my consciousness and the injured hand. When I momentarily passed mentally through that wall, I felt the injury extremely; so I was perfectly willing to remain behind that wall! There was a little fear in my mind that someone would come in contact with my hand, so I held it across my chest inside my coat; and that was all I did. That evening a party of us were to attend a performance at the Hollywood Bowl; so complete was the Guru's healing care, I was able to go along with the group.

"The next day I had breakfast and dinner with the Master, but he paid no attention to my trouble. I was satisfied to leave it that way, and say nothing. That evening I left by train for the East, still without referring to the injury; that wall around my consciousness was still there. The following morning at breakfast I had courage enough to look at my hand. The fingers were normal in shape and size. All that remained of the injury was a little blue discoloration on two fingers; there was no discomfort. This was an instance of almost instantaneous healing of matter. The Master's strong mind, contacting God's power, had prevented the pattern of injury from being accepted by my mind. Thus I was saved from much difficulty and pain. Mind coupled with God's consciousness and power can do anything. It has created our bodies; therefore it can change our bodies."

"I Never Missed in My Practice of *Kriya Yoga*"

Dr. Lewis was master of ceremonies at the Self-Realization Fellowship Convocation in Los Angeles in August 1951. He said:

"Paramahansaji showed me the great light of God, and told me: 'If you cling to this path and regularly meditate, this vision will be your own always.' And so I followed his advice. I never missed in my practice of *Kriya*

Dr. Lewis and Sri Prabhas Chandra Ghosh, vice president, Yogoda Satsanga Society of India; at welcoming ceremonies, international headquarters, April 14, 1954

Dr. Lewis with a bouquet of freshly plucked dates for his guru Paramahansa Yoganandaji *(right)*; Phoenix, Arizona, November 1948

Yoga. Gradually the light of God came in. What I received, I received from the Master. He lifted me from the uncertainty of delusion into the light of Reality. When that experience comes it changes the heart. Then we feel the real brotherhood of man and the Fatherhood of God.

"Mrs. Lewis had a coronary thrombosis. Through the grace of God working through the Guru, she was completely healed. Many who know her can assure you of that.

"Self-Realization teachings give you the realization of the Infinite Light whence all things come. Do your *Kriya* regularly. You will realize the allness of God, and in His omnipresence nothing inharmonious can touch you. As the Master often says, 'You can stand unshaken amidst the crash of breaking worlds.'"

At a *Kriya Yoga* initiation on August 25, 1951, during the Convocation, Gurudeva announced that Dr. Lewis and several other disciples might henceforth use the title *Yogacharya* (teacher of yoga).

With Paramahansaji on His Last Birthday, in Los Angeles

At Sri Yogananda's birthday celebration, January 5, 1952, just two months before he left his body, the Master and Dr. Lewis exchanged the banter about their respective ages that had become traditional on these occasions. (Both were born in 1893.) Doctor hinted that he was going to reveal the Guru's age, and Paramahansaji feigned consternation. Then he said:

"I see [by the single candle on the cake] my age is one—my age is infinite. So it is wonderful to have one candle!" Childlike, he added, "Shall I blow it out?"

Doctor teasingly replied, "If you can, yes!" Paramahansaji laughed and said: "I think I still have a little strength of breath!"

Doctor then read to the assemblage some of the telegrams of congratulation that had poured in from centers and individual students all over the world.

On January 10 the Guru traveled to Encinitas. He arranged a special dinner in the Hermitage, to which he invited Rajarsi, the Lewises, and a few other disciples. It was Paramahansaji's last visit to the Encinitas Ashram, founded by him in 1937.

Then Gurudeva departed for his desert retreat in Twentynine Palms, California. Doctor and Mrs. Lewis visited him there. In the quietude of the desert, he and Doctor had their last long talk. Paramahansaji said:

"Remember the good times we had in the beginning? As we started,

The ambassador of India, B. R. Sen *(right)*, and the Consul General of India, M. R. Ahuja, with Dr. Lewis at Self-Realization Fellowship International Headquarters, Los Angeles, March 4, 1952

Dr. Lewis, Brother Premamoy, the Shankaracharya of Puri, India, and his aide C. M. Trivedi, during the Shankaracharya's visit to Self-Realization Fellowship Ashram, Encinitas, February 1958

so let us finish. Life is just a dream. Where is your father? Where is my father? They are gone; but the love that we felt in the beginning is the same. We'll be apart a little, then together again."

The Peerless Guru Enters *Mahasamadhi*

Paramahansaji returned to Los Angeles on March 1, 1952. Three days later he entertained at the Self-Realization International Headquarters the Ambassador of India, Mr. Binay Ranjan Sen, and Mme. Sen. The Lewises were present.

On the night of March 7, at a banquet held at the Biltmore Hotel in honor of the Ambassador, the peerless Guru entered *mahasamadhi* (a great yogi's final conscious exit from the body).

The Lewises, after receiving the heartbreaking news, hastened from Encinitas to Los Angeles, arriving in the small hours of the morning to join the other grieving disciples.

Rajarsi Janakananda (James J. Lynn), Paramahansaji's successor as president of SRF-YSS, and Dr. Lewis conducted the partly Vedic, partly Christian ascension ceremonies for Guruji on March 11 at the international headquarters. Ambassador Sen and Consul M. R. Ahuja attended the funeral. "Death has no victory in him," Mr. Sen said.

Faithfully Carrying On the Work

The SRF Hollywood Ashram Center, another of the "big places," celebrated its first anniversary on April 7, 1952. Rajarsi and Dr. Lewis took leading parts in the festive proceedings. In July of the same year Doctor assisted Rajarsi in conducting services and classes at the Convocation.

Monks of the Self-Realization Order convened on December 23 at the Encinitas Hermitage for the annual Christmas meditation, with Rajarsi and Dr. Lewis presiding; nuns of the Order meditated in the chapel at the Mother Center with Sri Daya Mata.

In a sermon at the temple in San Diego in 1952, Doctor told the following story—one that illustrates the Lord's willingness to fulfill a devotee's desires:

"This was demonstrated to me once," Dr. Lewis said, "when I was first with Paramahansaji, and meditating a great deal. I used to sit in meditation trying to understand how the energy is withdrawn from the body, how the sense perceptions are withdrawn, and how to leave the body consciousness and get into the realm of spiritual things, into superconsciousness. I knew how in theory, and I was able to feel I was not the

The Lewises in Encinitas, May 1955

body consciousness; but I had not experienced the withdrawing of energy from the involuntary nerves. Then one day when I was meditating deeply, I felt my body become as cold as ice, with perspiration all over it. I was fully conscious. Something prompted me to feel the top of my head. It was almost as hot as a stove. This showed me beyond a doubt that the top of the head is the place where the energy leaves the body and merges in the surrounding cosmic energy. Now I could have read about that all my life without actually knowing it. But God answered my desire to know by giving me that experience, so I could realize the truth and not just theorize about it. The Lord truly does answer us if we make the effort and give our devotion to Him....

"If we can understand that God speaks to us in these various ways, indirectly and directly, it should not be difficult for us to comprehend that we can sometimes hear Him speak in a voice audible to our physical ears; and even in words, as He spoke to me when I was a little boy. In God's consciousness are all the senses—sight, touch, hearing, and the others; everything is in His divine consciousness, not in the physical body. The sense of hearing is not in the ear; it is in the divine consciousness of God, which projected the body. The same is true of sight, touch, taste, and smell. God can produce, through the Holy Ghost Vibration,* any manifestation, any sound,

*Known in Hindu scriptures as *Aum.* The Bible refers to "the Comforter, which is the Holy Ghost" (John 14:26) and "the Word" — the cosmic vibration of God's power that upholds all creation.

perceptible to our outward consciousness.

Hearing, in the Guru's Presence, the Astral Bee-Sound

"Sometimes such a sound is audible not only to our own ears but to the ears of others. On one such occasion, when some of the disciples were with Master at the Encinitas Hermitage, we heard the bee sound, which emanates from the coccygeal center of the spine.* This humming was audible to our ears clear across the room from where Paramahansaji was sitting.

"Another instance of hearing the bee sound quite audibly took place when some of us were in San Francisco in 1939 attending the Golden Gate International Exposition. Master and I and the others were reminiscing one night, way into the morning hours, as we usually did; and as we were sitting there I suddenly heard the bee sound. Master chuckled and said, 'Listen.' We could hear it quite a few feet away, and we were hearing with our ordinary ears; we weren't in meditation at all. The Divine Consciousness was speaking to us through plainly audible sound."

Doctor Was a Gracious Host and a Welcome Guest

On June 14, 1953, Dr. and Mrs. Lewis and a large number of other Self-Realization students were invited to attend a banquet at Hotel Statler in Los Angeles in honor of Dr. Sarvepalli Radhakrishnan, Vice President of the Republic of India.

The Ambassador of India, Mr. G. L. Mehta, visited Self-Realization Fellowship International Headquarters on October 23. The Lewises presided over the welcoming ceremonies. The Ambassador observed, "You keep the Master's tradition very well."†

The next evening Dr. and Mrs. Lewis were guests of honor at the speakers' table at a banquet for Ambassador Mehta in the Biltmore Hotel.

A large Christmas banquet for Self-Realization students was given on December 21 at the Hollywood Ashram's India Hall. Dr. Lewis was among the speakers on this happy occasion. In his talk he paid touching tribute to his Guru, and to the extraordinary value of Self-Realization Fellowship teachings. His words were, as always, reassuring to the devotees, who still felt keenly the terrestrial absence of

*One of the subtle spinal centers, located at the base of the spine. The subtle astral sounds emanating from the spinal centers can be heard through practice of a certain meditation technique taught in the *Self-Realization Fellowship Lessons.*

†The tradition of Indian hospitality—"The guest is God."

Dr. M. W. Lewis *(center)* at an informal discussion with monks of the Self-Realization Order, in lounge of first Self-Realization Fellowship Retreat, Encinitas, California, Christmas Eve, 1957

Dr. M. W. Lewis *(second from right)* and Mrs. Lewis *(fifth from left)* among the guests of honor at a banquet for Mr. G. L. Mehta, Ambassador of India; Biltmore Hotel, Los Angeles, October 24, 1953

Paramahansaji. A few extracts from Doctor's talk follow:

"The Love of God Is Real"

"Through a little meditation and the grace of the Master and God, I can testify that the love of God is real; it is substantial. It will mean more to you than anything that money can buy....Guruji always said, 'Religion is not a superficial thing. The practice of true religion will make you happy.' Without the personal experience of God, which is true religion, our lives are empty of real happiness. Not all the gifts and comforts of the world can fill the void.

"Jesus told his disciples that although he would not be with them, still he would leave them the Comforter, and that in the Comforter they would find answers to all their questions. Paramahansaji, like Jesus, has left us the comfort of the Holy Ghost, the great light of the Cosmic Intelligent Vibration spread through all creation. He is one with it. He gave us the ways and means to merge ourselves in it. From its light we have been created. In that light we are sustained. And into that light we shall finally melt again.

"It is true that the divine light seems to be hidden. But if you persevere in meditation as the Master has taught, there is a great surprise in store for you. God will come. That light of God can be known by us because Master came as a special divine dispensation to show all people, regardless of race or creed, how they can be one with that light. Through *Kriya* Paramahansaji has given us the power to know that great light, to realize it as a living reality.

"We must get rid of the ego, that the light of God which was manifest in the Master can flow freely into us. When God comes in, you realize that He alone is the Doer. Then you can truly help people, because you will have realization. The Holy Ghost goes from you to them, and that is something real. Words will be unnecessary. Keep on. Meditate deeply. Then that light of the Master will be with you to such an extent that nothing else will matter to you. 'If God be for us, who can be against us?'* God is with us. The Master is with us. All is well."

When the Hollywood Ashram Center celebrated its third anniversary in 1954, Doctor was again on hand to deliver a brief address, and to inspire the congregation with selections on the organ. He was a spiritual "fixture" at all such annual celebrations, and will ever be sorely missed at these functions by all who knew and loved him.

* Romans 8:31.

Dr. Lewis *(left)* greets Sri Prabhas Ghosh, vice president of Yogoda Satsanga Society of India, after Encinitas Ashram renunciants had showered the honored guest with rose petals, April 15, 1954.

Dr. Lewis *(fourth from left)* and SRF members at a birthday commemoration service for Paramahansa Yogananda, January 5, 1960, in Encinitas Hermitage. Mrs. Lewis *(in white)* stands near garlanded photograph of Sri Yogananda.

The year 1954 was an unusually busy one for the Lewises. Yogoda Satsanga Society representatives from India, including Paramahansaji's cousin, Sri Prabhas Chandra Ghosh, vice president of YSS in India, came to America for two months. On April 14, Sri Daya Mata, Dr. Lewis, and a large group of other Self-Realizationists welcomed the honored guests at the international headquarters with elaborate India-style ceremonies. The following day the Indians visited Rajarsi and the Lewises at the Encinitas Ashram. The guests made trips to nearby points of interest where Paramahansaji had liked to go, such as the San Diego Zoo and the Palomar Observatory. The Lewises accompanied the Indian devotees on several occasions.

Doctor Lewis Presided at Many Self-Realization Functions

In August there were classes and ceremonies to conduct during the 1954 Convocation. Doctor presided at the Rose Ceremony, a simple rite of devotion to God that Paramahansaji had taught the students during the early days in Boston. At that time it was celebrated annually as the Yogoda Festival.

In December Doctor assumed joyous Christmastime duties, when he presided at the monks' Christmas meditation and banquet at the Encinitas Ashram Center.

On February 20, 1955, Rajarsi Janakananda passed on. The funeral rites were held three days later at the Church of the Recessional, Forest Lawn Memorial-Park, Glendale. After a eulogy delivered by Sri Daya Mata, Dr. Lewis spoke.

"Rajarsi Janakananda lived engrossed in the light and love of the Infinite Father," Doctor said, "an illumination bestowed on him through the channel of our beloved master Paramahansa Yogananda. Only with the language of our hearts may we pay fitting tribute to Rajarsi. And that language is the unconditional divine love we feel for him."

Two years earlier Dr. Lewis had started at the Hollywood Ashram Center a Friday-evening class for monks. In 1955 another class was added on Friday evenings, for lay disciples from the Los Angeles area; this group met immediately after the monks' class. The lay devotees' two-hour meeting included meditation and chanting. Doctor often played the organ to accompany the group singing. He presided over these two Friday-evening gatherings uninterruptedly until a month before his passing.

The Friday-evening meditations begun by Dr. Lewis for the lay disciples are still attended devotedly by the Los Angeles members.

A Spiritual "Shot" Heard Round the World

As Paramahansaji had predicted, the work continued to grow with the passing years. In 1957 Self-Realization Fellowship held its largest Convocation up to that time. At the garden party on August 11 Dr. Lewis led the invocation. "I was just thinking," he concluded, "of a garden party held by our beloved Master in Lexington, Massachusetts, in June 1921. Lexington, you know, is the place where the shot was fired that was 'heard round the world.' And so I was thinking that Paramahansaji's establishing Self-Realization Fellowship in 1920 was a spiritual 'shot' that is being heard round the world, too. Today there are six hundred of us assembled here. There were only thirty-five or forty of us at that Lexington garden party; but I remember with what love and protection he looked at us then. And I know he looks down on us now with that same love and care."

Tribute to Self-Realizationists by Sri Shankaracharya

In 1958 His Holiness Sri Shankaracharya Sri Jagadguru Bharati Krishna Tirtha of the three-thousand-year-old Gowardhan Math in Puri, India, paid a three-months' visit to America under the sponsorship of Self-Realization Fellowship. It was the first time in the history of the

Swami Order that a Shankaracharya had visited the West. His Holiness spent some weeks at the international headquarters, where on many occasions he talked on spiritual subjects with Sri Daya Mata and other ashram residents. He also traveled to Encinitas, where he stayed for a short time, and enjoyed meeting the Lewises and other ashram members. After he had returned to India, Sri Shankaracharya said:

"I found in Self-Realization Fellowship the highest spirituality, service, and love. Not only do its representatives preach these principles, but they live according to them."

Doctor Valiantly Carried a Heavy Schedule to the End

Dr. Lewis served Paramahansaji's work with unchanging enthusiasm. To the end of his days he kept a heavy schedule of classes and services, traveling back and forth each week between his home in Encinitas and the temples in San Diego and Hollywood. He was also frequently called upon, in his capacity as vice president, to preside at various ceremonies and to represent Self-Realization Fellowship at important public meetings.

His administrative duties in connection with the Encinitas Ashram Center, and various special assignments he undertook at the request of the Board of Directors, were considerable. He also gave generously of his time to Self-Realization Fellowship students who sought counsel on the teachings. The strain showed physically, and his fellow disciples expressed loving concern for his welfare. But the spiritual zeal that had kept him "in harness" all these years enabled him to fulfill his great desire to be "faithful unto death."*

Greatest of all, Doctor remained faithful to his search for ever higher heights of God-realization through *Kriya Yoga*. The following words of Paramahansa Yogananda, which describe what happens at death, should inspire others to follow the example of Dr. Lewis as a *Kriya Yogi*. Paramahansaji said:

"When a person dies, as the life force in the body goes up through the spine and out through the thousand-rayed lotus in the top of the head to merge in the Cosmic Life Force, it enlivens all the little films of past experiences that are stored in the subconscious mind, and you see your whole life spread before you. If you have made God your own during this life, there will be no break in continuity of consciousness as you go out of the body. If you have lived a materialistic life, you will

* "Be thou faithful unto death, and I will give thee a crown of life" (Revelation 2:10).

Dr. Lewis offering prayer before picnic lunch on grounds of Encinitas Ashram Center, August 24, 1953, during visit by some of the members who attended the 1953 Self-Realization Fellowship Convocation

have to review it all painfully; but if you have developed your soul consciousness, you will slip through death into the great light of God; and the subconscious revelation of all you have done during this life will neither affect nor disturb you. You will realize that your life was only a part in a play, that you are and ever have been one with God."

An Exit in the True Yogic Tradition

Doctor Lewis made his exit in the true yogic tradition, demonstrating with his last breath what devotion to God, Guru, and *Kriya Yoga* can do for loyal followers of the Self-Realization path.

Dear Doctor, your fellow disciples can well believe Gurudeva's beautiful words to you: that the candles you lighted in your Father's house while you were here will light your way hereafter.

DR. MINOTT W. LEWIS

This photograph was taken at Self-Realization Fellowship International Headquarters, Los Angeles, on November 27, 1956.

In 1946 Paramahansaji had presented Dr. and Mrs. Lewis with a copy of his *Autobiography of a Yogi,* in which he had written:

"Through your ever-deep loyalty to God, the Gurus, *Kriya Yoga,* and to me, and your glowing service to Self-Realization Fellowship, you have secured your passport to heaven and to the deepest recesses of my heart."

The Last Days of Doctor Lewis

BY MILDRED LEWIS

On Sunday, March 20, 1960, Dr. Lewis held his last service at Self-Realization Temple in Hollywood; and his last Sunday-night meditation service at the retreat chapel in Encinitas. The following day, in his apartment in the Hermitage, Doctor kept many appointments with students. Though Doctor never spoke of his illness to others, our daughter Brenda and I noticed that he seemed very tired. On Tuesday morning he and I motored to our desert retreat in Borrego Springs, where he could have a restful change.

While there, he seemed different: an outward sparkle and enthusiasm were gone. An atmosphere of remoteness surrounded him.

On Thursday, March 24, we returned to Encinitas. That afternoon Dr. Lewis saw his physician, who had been treating Doctor for heart trouble. The physician ordered two weeks of complete rest.

Dr. Lewis, however, had several engagements that he felt constrained to keep. After supper that day he held his last Thursday-evening class at the Hermitage. The following day he conducted the funeral rites for a Self-Realization student. On Sunday, March 27, he spoke at the temple in San Diego. The following Sunday, April 3, he gave his last sermon there. This was his last public appearance.

It was not easy for Doctor to rest; his temperament was too active. Often we would urge him to heed his physician's instructions. "Remember," Brenda would tell him, "you can get along without us, but we can't get along without you." With a sweet smile Doctor would say soothingly: "I understand."

As his condition was not improving, on April 7 his physician ordered him to enter Scripps Memorial Hospital in La Jolla for a rest and medical tests. Doctor had a lovely room there—private, quiet, overlooking the ocean. Each day Brenda would visit him in the morning; then I would go in the afternoon and stay with him until the closing hour for visitors.

The first three days in the hospital were hard on him, because of the tests. On Monday, however, he seemed greatly improved. On the following day he said he felt well enough to go home.

When Brenda returned home from the hospital on Wednesday, April 13, she seemed distressed. (Later she told me that during the morning visit her father, though loving as always, appeared distant and withdrawn.)

I went immediately to the hospital and found Doctor resting comfortably. That day we had such a pleasant time together! After his supper, which he enjoyed, he sat in a chair for thirteen minutes and then returned to bed. At seven p.m. he said he would take a nap. He slept very peacefully until seven-thirty, when he awakened and told me, "I want to sit up straight." I arranged the pillows at his back as he assumed the lotus pose for his usual evening meditation. His hands were upturned, his eyes closed. I sat beside the bed, thinking that I too would meditate.

I was aroused in two or three minutes by a tremendous sound. It resembled the suction sound of a huge pump, or the breath sound of a giant *Kriya.* With the sound came a great flash of spiritual white light, whose brilliance might be compared to that given forth by a million electric-light bulbs.

Doctor's blue eyes opened; piercing flashes of blue light came from them. Then they were locked at the Christ center in the forehead. His head lowered somewhat, but his body remained erect. For an instant, the face of Swami Sri Yukteswarji appeared, enveloping Doctor's face. Then all was over.

How many times I have thanked God, the Great Ones, and beloved Master that I was privileged to witness such a glorious passing!

Mrs. Lewis and Doctor at SRF International Headquarters, November 27, 1956

Eulogy at Dr. Lewis's Funeral

Sri Daya Mata, president of Self-Realization Fellowship/Yogoda Satsanga Society of India, conducted the final rites for Dr. Lewis on April 18, 1960, at Church of the Recessional, Forest Lawn Memorial-Park, Glendale, California.

Five hundred mourners attended the service. The body of Doctor Lewis was interred at Forest Lawn near the "Court of David."

Parts of Sri Daya Mata's speech follow.

It is with sad hearts that we meet here today to pay homage to our beloved Doctor Lewis. We of the monastic Self-Realization Order have lost a devoted and faithful brother disciple of our guru, Paramahansa Yogananda; and all members of Self-Realization Fellowship have lost a dear friend and counselor. We cannot but grieve over our personal loss; yet we rejoice for him in his reunion with our blessed Gurudeva.

Dr. Lewis met Paramahansaji in Boston on Christmas Eve, 1920, shortly after Guruji had arrived in America to speak as the delegate from India at an International Congress of Religious Liberals. You all have doubtless heard some of the stirring tales of those early years—years when Master was struggling to spread his divine mission; years during which Doctor and Mildred, his wife, gave generous assistance to the young monk from India; years in which they shared together many dreams for the future of the work.

Dr. Lewis was one of the first disciples of Paramahansaji in this country. It was in Boston that Gurudeva established his first meditation center. Later, in 1923, when he went to New York, he left Dr. Lewis in charge of that center.

Years passed, during which Doctor and Master kept in touch regularly. Paramahansaji established the international headquarters in Los Angeles in 1925, and from time to time guru and disciple met—either when Master returned to Boston, in the course of his lecture engagements, or when Dr. and Mrs. Lewis visited Guruji's ashrams in southern California.

I would like to read to you now a poem written to Dr. Lewis by Paramahansaji in Phoenix, Arizona, on February 7, 1930:

"What I feel about our friendship I spontaneously write:

Flowers sent by loving Self-Realizationists from many parts of the world surround casket of Dr. Lewis at funeral service, April 18, 1960, Church of the Recessional, Forest Lawn Memorial-Park, Glendale, California

"God, I care not for riches
Nor for fame or pomp;
But give me true friends!
Even just one, if it be he
Through whom I may behold Thee
And whom I may trust and enjoy without, as Thine image,
E'er reflected in the mirror of my love.

"A friend is he who feels my direst needs as his own,
Who feels for me as he would feel for himself.

"Ah, wavelets of true friendship, heaven-born,
Merge in Thy one ocean of vast Love!
In the sea of friendship
The meandering lost and prodigal souls
Come back to their own one home."

I remember my own first meeting with Dr. Lewis in 1933 in Chicago. I had gone there, along with other disciples, to attend the World Fellowship of Faiths lectures at the World's Fair, where Paramahansaji was to speak. I recall the instantaneous recognition that passed between Dr. Lewis and me, as memories buried in the heap of previous lives flooded our consciousness.

I have dear recollections of those wonderful, carefree days in the late 1940s, after Dr. and Mrs. Lewis had come to live in Encinitas. How sweet were those days when we sat around Master, listening to him expound the truths that show the basic unity of all great religions! At times Doctor and I would hold lively philosophical discussions—for example, on the question of whether or not suffering is necessary for salvation. The blessed Guru's eyes would twinkle as he encouraged us to continue, while he himself remained withdrawn.

Memories crowd in, too, of the weekly picnics with Gurudeva in the nearby mountain quiet, ending with a session of deep meditation and a quiet drive homeward. Memories, memories! of so many wonderful experiences shared with our beloved brother disciple Dr. Lewis.

After the passing of our second president, Rajarsi Janakananda, Dr. Lewis assumed the directorship of our ashram center in Encinitas and there continued his ministry, speaking regularly also in our Hollywood and San Diego temples. In all these places he had an earnest and devoted following.

Upon my return from India late in 1959 I noted the seeming weariness of our revered Doctor. I reminded him, as I had on earlier occasions, that he should relinquish some of his duties. He replied, "Yes, yes, I will think about it." But his heart and mind had long been dedicated to tireless service, and he continued his selfless activity. He had but one wish—to live constantly in the consciousness of his divine Guru and his supreme God, and to impart something of that spiritual ardor to those who came to him. His sudden passing was a great shock to all of us, and my heart is sorely grieved over our loss.

The end was wreathed in divine glory. Doctor had entered Scripps Memorial Hospital in La Jolla a few days before, merely for a rest and a check-up. Only the day before his death, Mildred, his beloved wife, had written me to say that he was much improved; and we all felt greatly encouraged. He seemed even better on the day of his passing, she tells us. Mildred was alone with him at his bedside that evening. He took a little supper, and then fell into a light sleep.

When he awoke he sat up and arranged his body in the lotus posture for meditation. Sitting cross-legged on the bed, his eyes upturned toward the Christ center in the forehead, Doctor became enveloped in an aura of profound peace. Suddenly, Mildred tells us, the whole room became radiant; Sri Yukteswarji's face appeared. Doctor's eyes were like two pools

Paramahansa Yogananda *(left)* with Dr. Lewis opening gifts at Paramahansaji's birthday celebration, January 5, 1952

of dazzling blue light. With a look of majesty and power, he was gone.

Thus passed Doctor—a beloved brother disciple, a faithful servant and friend of our great Master. By his example Doctor inspired many men and women to seek the Divine. We cannot forget him—the sweet simplicity of his life, his untiring spirit of service, and his great love for God and Guru. May he inspire each one of us to use the term of life yet allotted to us to strive ever more earnestly, devoutly, with humility and love in our hearts, to seek and serve the Beloved of the Universe, to whom all Self-Realizationists have dedicated their lives—whether as renunciants in our ashrams or as householder-yogis in the world.

In conclusion I will read to you a soul-stirring extract from a letter written to Dr. Lewis by Paramahansaji in New York, dated Nov. 23, 1923:

"Be not afraid, child of the Eternal Lightning! March on with unperturbed, steady steps, elbowing your way through a million darknesses. Why, what is the body? what is this passing show? They are soon gone; but the candles that you are lighting and burning in your Father's house will show you your path here and hereafter."

Going Home

By Minott W. Lewis

Creeping inward, creeping upward,
Diving deep within, we find
Treasures lasting and uplifting;
Best of all, that Peace sublime.

Many lives we've spent in serving
Senses, passions, and mind's whim,
And have missed our own true being—
Oneness with the God within.

Let us therefore give this one life
To the fight for higher gain;
With the hope, when life stops ebbing,
That the task was not in vain.

O Great God, above in heaven!
Hear our cry, we pray, tonight;
Keep us steadfast in Thy wisdom,
Keep us always in Thy light.

O RING OF GOLD!

By Minott W. Lewis

There comes a time in each one's life
When he must turn e'er left or right.
Two roads diverge. Stop! Take your choice.
One leads to Darkness, one to Light.

Matter, grand display will play
To lure you to her endless ray.
Be not misled, her path to try:
"Whoe'er treads here can never die."

Eternal Life will still be lost,
For thou hast yet to pay the cost.
Go, look within; still Matter's din;
Perfect thyself whilst search for Him.

With fullest love for Him begin
With all thy heart, thy will, and limb;
And soon thou'lt find the strangest Spy—
Not "I", but I, for "I" hath died.

In breathless silence back you'll creep
With none to guide save great *Om*'s beat.
Within that *Om,* thine age-long Friend
Whose guidance will be till the end.

O ring of gold! within, a nameless hue;
O door of heaven! by which we all pass through
Into that realm, God's kingdom bright—
Eternal Bliss, Immortal Light.

LAST PHOTOGRAPH OF DR. LEWIS

This picture of Doctor, smiling yet introspective, was taken at Self-Realization Fellowship Temple, San Diego, California, February 7, 1960.

Dr. Lewis presiding at Sunday service, Self-Realization Fellowship Temple, San Diego, California, February 7, 1960

Dr. Lewis chats with youngest resident of Self-Realization Fellowship Ashram Center in Encinitas, May 1955.

Tributes to Dr. Lewis

Received at SRF Headquarters after his passing

"I have precious memories of my brother disciple, Dr. Lewis. He shone as a *Kriya Yogi* on earth, and is now a greater light in heaven."—*Yogacharya J. Oliver Black, SRF Center, Detroit, Michigan*

"Many of us had the privilege and great blessing of knowing Dr. Lewis and of hearing his sermons in Encinitas, San Diego, and Hollywood; and of attending his classes at Convocations. All of us who knew him loved him."—*Yogacharya J. M. Cuaron, SRF Center, Mexico City, Mexico*

"We at Yogoda Math mourn the passing of beloved Dr. Lewis. I cherish memories of his kindness and hospitality in Encinitas. We held a loving memorial service for him on April 18."—*Sri Prabhas Chandra Ghosh, vice president, Yogoda Satsanga Society of India*

"We in New Zealand had not the pleasure of meeting Dr. Lewis, but from the record of his activities and from his articles in the magazine we have come to hold him in very high regard. We are happy in the knowledge that he has graduated to a higher calling in the service he loved so well. Customarily, we talk of 'loss,' yet one does feel that these passings strengthen the chain of spiritual-supply lines extending through to the highest center. We joy in all we have been taught by the beloved Master and his disciples, and find that experience in God Consciousness in which we feel the continuing presence of all our beloved Brethren. This gives us a sense of a still more strengthened link cementing a great and grand infinite family in love and understanding. God blesses the passing of Dr. Lewis, and we welcome yet another established Light beckoning us on to Reality."—*SRF Center, Auckland, New Zealand*

"We know of Doctor Lewis's life of purity and his dedication to the highest ideals of SRF. No doubt his noble heart will ever be sending vibrations of loving helpfulness from the invisible places to all those who look to Self-Realization Fellowship for aid, guidance, comforting, and salvation. Our meditation this evening will be conducted for the peace of his soul."—*SRF Center, Caracas, Venezuela*

"Though one should understand all phenomena in the way our Heavenly Father expects of us, nevertheless it is sad to hear of the death of Dr. Lewis—one who was so close to Master. After Paramahansaji's passing, Dr. Lewis wrote me a very kind little note. I shall keep it always. Whenever I hear of any of Master's disciples passing over, I always imagine Paramahansaji's meeting him or her, and making himself perfectly recognizable. I pray ever that I too shall have just that experience."—*Secretary, SRF Center, London, England*

"News of Dr. Lewis's death has been received with great sorrow. We are all bereaved."—*SRF Center, Takoradi, Ghana, Africa*

"One of the very first disciples of Paramahansaji in the United States has joined his Guru and the saintly souls of Sister Gyanamata and Rajarsi Janakananda. Though the loss of Dr. Lewis is deeply felt by all, it divinely inspires us to greater effort towards fulfillment of our sacred pledge to our blessed Guru."—*SRF Center, Sydney, Australia*

"We are very sorry to learn of the passing of Dr. Lewis; this great disciple worked hard, hand in hand with our great Guru, since the dawn of Yoga teaching in America."—*SRF Center, Monterrey, Mexico*

"We sorrow because of the earth-exit of that great soul, Dr. M. W. Lewis. Those of us who had the great privilege of meeting him and receiving his guidance specially feel that a living example of our Guru's teachings has been outwardly lost for the organization. However, he can now shed on us more light from higher planes; in that sense, everyone has gained."—*SRF Center, Cali, Colombia*

"I know the Board will miss Dr. Lewis, as it could always rely on him to carry out his responsibilities. Thousands of people will miss him. His tolerant, kindly understanding was a powerful magnet."—*D.B.T., Eastbourne, England*

"One more 'rare flower in God's garden,' may Dr. Lewis feel our gratitude returning to him as a continual blessing."—*T. K., Germany*

"Doctor will always live in my heart as a great example of Master's teachings and as a true friend. I know that there are many who feel as I do and who, like myself, have benefited spiritually by knowing him."—*D. R., Niantic, Connecticut*

"Doctor's unswerving loyalty to God and his Guru was indeed exemplary. His great example lit a flame of devotion to God in the hearts of many of Master Yogananda's disciples."—*A. L., Los Angeles, California*

"We know that dear Doctor will have a beautiful well-deserved 'mansion' in the Father's kingdom. He was one of the saintliest men I ever met, a wonderful soul with a single eye, strong in his belief and yet so gentle."—*A. S., Rancho Santa Fe, California*

"Surely if he had been able to dictate the exact manner of his passing it would have been just as it was—a swift escape while mind and soul were attuned to their Source. Heaped on this victory was that immense offering of love, almost tangible, whereby hundreds who attended the funeral services returned to his soul a part of what he had freely given to them."—*V. S., Los Angeles, California*

"Life is short; eternity is long. Dr. Lewis knew this when, many years ago, he exchanged the desire of material things for the spiritual ones that last."—*C. M., New York, New York*

"I am deeply saddened to learn of the death of Dr. Lewis. I have lost a great, dear friend! He helped me during all these years by his every word. His love, goodness, and humility can be an example to all of us."—*R. A., Rome, Italy*

"I shall always pray I may have the courage, faith, and loyalty that Doctor had. It is through devotees like him that we newer ones gain strength."—*M. B., Los Angeles, California*

"What a time he and Master must be having! I never think of them apart."—*Y. B., Encinitas, California*

"I have rarely experienced such tears of joy as when I read the life of Dr. Lewis in *Self-Realization* magazine. It is rewarding to see a Westerner so blessed not only by the *Kriya Yoga* technique but also by the guidance of the Master Paramahansa Yoganandaji."—*G. H., St. Paul, Minnesota*

"The service at Forest Lawn was full of love and devotion for Doctor, who was the instrument for so many to know God. He was a true religious teacher."—*L.W.E., South Duxbury, Massachusetts*

"A wonderfully kind, tolerant, understanding, sympathetic, reliable, and highly evolved soul—Dr. Lewis."—*D. T., England*

"I thank God and Guru for the privilege of knowing Dr. Lewis. I talked with him many times; he would always see me, if but for a minute. I owe him a deep debt. In his presence I have been healed of headaches, colds, and mental miseries. He was my friend, a true lover of God."—*J.O.N., Bellflower, California*

Mildred M. Lewis

A Memorial Tribute

Mildred M. Lewis, faithful and beloved disciple of Paramahansa Yogananda for sixty-eight years, passed away at the age of ninety on March 30, 1988, at her residence on the grounds of the Self-Realization Fellowship Temple, San Diego, California.

She was born in Boston in 1897, but spent her early childhood in New Hampshire. Her family moved back to Massachusetts when she was seven. There, in Duxbury, she became acquainted with her future husband and lifetime companion, Minott W. Lewis.

The following is a condensation of Mrs. Lewis's memorial service—a loving farewell to this disciple who is loved and respected by SRF members and friends around the world. The service was conducted at Forest Lawn Memorial-Park, Los Angeles, by Sri Mrinalini Mata, then vice president of Self-Realization Fellowship.

It is said that when a liberated master comes to earth to accomplish a divinely ordained mission, he brings with him disciples from past incarnations to help him. So it was with our blessed guru, Paramahansa Yogananda. When the time came for him to establish his work worldwide, he sailed across the sea from India to a foreign land where he knew no one; but the silent call of his soul had gone ahead of him. Among the very first to respond were Dr. and Mrs. M. W. Lewis—Doctor and Mildred. What a comfort it must have been for Master to see these familiar faces he had known in lives past; to find these divine friends who would help him in his mission. It was a symbol that his work in the West would succeed.

Today, sixty-eight years later, our hearts are full with loving thoughts of our dear Mildred. One cannot even begin to sum up in a few minutes a life of ninety years—particularly a life in which nearly seven decades were spent as a devoted, faithful disciple of an avatar, a divine incarnation. And that was only one of many roles for many people that Mildred played in this life. As a dedicated, exemplary mother, she earned the lifelong devotion of her two children, J. Bradford Lewis and Brenda Rosser, as well as that of her six grandchildren and four great-grandchildren and other family members.

An Example of the Ideal Householder Life

As wife, Mildred strove with Doctor to live that perfect householder life exemplified by Lahiri Mahasaya.* He was their ideal. Through their many years of seeking and serving God together, Doctor and Mildred have been an example on this path of Self-Realization of how husband and wife should be loyal, dedicated, and devoted to each other through thick and thin, helping one another along the path to God.

They were divine companions, and their divergent natures blended in a perfect balance. Doctor was the philosopher; he was always more interested in the world of Spirit than in the world of matter. Mildred was more the pragmatist; she understood that in this world of relativity, man cannot live by Spirit alone. The wisdom of her soul expressed as a down-to-earth, practical grasp of affairs; and Gurudeva loved that quality in her. He often said, "She has a very keen mind. I can always talk with her; I can always reason with her. She understands me."

Mildred Was a Divine Friend to Countless Souls

The world can little know nor understand fully the depths of divine friendship. Master spoke often of this to us. When the love of God flowing through the guru touches the hearts of disciples near and dear to the master, a bond is formed among them that lasts through incarnations. We know that among Doctor and Mildred and all of the devotees who were close to Master in this lifetime, such a bond was forged many incarnations ago; and renewed in this life through Gurudeva's love. Each disciple has a God-assigned role to play as we walk in unity and harmony, "agreeing and disagreeing"† as may be necessary in fulfilling

* Guru of Paramahansa Yogananda's guru. A Christlike master who attained the highest union with God, Lahiri Mahasaya was also a family man with business responsibilities. His mission was to show the modern world—through the science of *Kriya Yoga*—the balanced path of communion with God and conscientious fulfillment of worldly duties.

† A phrase oft quoted by Paramahansaji from his poem "Friendship" in *Songs of the Soul:*

these roles, but always in a oneness of spirit untouched and never severed by any events in the eternal drama of delusion.

Mildred freely gave of her friendship to the many who sought her counsel and inspiration. In loving respect for her years on the path, there were those who endearingly called her "Mama Lewis." Countless are her friends around the world—those who knew her personally, and also those who knew of her because of her place in the history of our Guru's divine mission.

A Special Relationship With the Guru

As a disciple she was much loved by Gurudeva. The Guru's relationship with each disciple is special and unique. There was a warm friendship between Master and Doctor and Mildred.

Frequently Mildred explained, "In the beginning, we didn't know what a guru was. There were no *Self-Realization Fellowship Lessons,* no *Autobiography of a Yogi,* to teach us. To us, Master was a friend." Even as an understanding of the guru-disciple relationship developed, that sweet, informal friendship endured. Such an intimate relationship between an avatar and his close disciples is possible only in the presence of great divine love, understanding, and soul communion.

When Doctor and Mildred left Boston permanently to live and serve in our ashram in Encinitas, Master assigned to them the task of supervising the greenhouse where we grew papayas and, later on, flowers. This was one of the early projects initiated by Gurudeva to help finance his growing organization. I can remember often seeing Doctor and Mildred returning to the ashram late in the evening, covered with mud, having been in the hot, humid greenhouse all day. In the spirit of true discipleship, they were willing to do any task—no matter how menial—for the guru.*

"Friendship is noble, fruitful, holy / When two separate souls march in difference / Yet in harmony; agreeing and disagreeing, / Glowingly improving diversely...."

*During a Christmas gathering at the SRF Mother Center in 1983, Mrs. Lewis said: "I have great respect for all of Master's devotees who are doing so much to carry on his work, because the very first publication that Master sent out in the mail went from my dining room table in Boston. People could send us ten cents and we would mail them a little booklet that told all about Yogoda [Self-Realization teachings]. We have come a long way since then! And I have been able to watch and enjoy this growth. My life has truly been blessed, and anything and everything that I can ever do for Master's work, as long as I'm on earth, I want to do it."

Naturally, after a long day of toiling in the greenhouse, Mildred would sometimes be very weary. But if Master was in residence in Encinitas, he and Doctor would often engage in talks on philosophy—sometimes until late into the night. I remember one such evening. Master summoned me to the Lewises' room. He and Doctor had been absorbed in one of their long discussions. Mildred was sitting there quietly, apparently listening intently. But Master said, "Look, she's asleep." I wondered at this, since Mildred's eyes were wide open. Guruji motioned to Doctor to take a Kleenex tissue and twist it to a little point, and tickle Mildred's nose with it. Mildred woke with a start. Master said, "You know, for months she was fooling us; we thought she was listening to our discussions. But look, she's been sleeping." Mildred looked at me and said, "I had to teach myself to sleep with eyes open; because that was the only way I was ever going to get any rest!" We all laughed heartily. Mildred absorbed Master's love and wisdom by osmosis, and this she shared with many in these later years when Doctor was no longer present as the spokesman.

The Real Resurrection

Mildred lived a long and full life of ninety years, which in itself is an awesome accomplishment.* However, to each of us comes the time when the body must go. As Master expressed it so beautifully, "We are spumescent bubbles on the sea of God's consciousness. The bubbles play for a while on the surface and then disappear again into the sea."

I want to read a few extracts from a little note that Master wrote to Mildred at Mt. Washington in 1942. The Lewises had come from Boston to spend Christmas with Master. He wrote to her:

Dear Mildred,

This letter is a token of my joy at your presence here with us. For God

*In 1935, Mrs. Lewis suffered a severe coronary thrombosis. The doctors were not certain that she would recover, and one heart specialist told her: "If you follow my instructions *exactly,* you might last until 1939." Mrs. Lewis did as the doctors instructed, but continued to have heart problems.

Several years later, during a visit to the Self-Realization Fellowship International Headquarters, Paramahansaji said to her, "You're not comfortable, are you?" Mrs. Lewis admitted that her heart was still bothering her. The Master blessed her and gave her personal instruction on how to strengthen her heart. In a short time she was completely healed, and years later her cardiac specialist told her, "Your heartbeat is so unique that without even seeing you I could recognize it out of a thousand."

> you came to me and for God you must keep a strong, unceasing vigil. Redouble, triple your efforts for God. Don't demand, but remember, God knows if you badly want Him. And when the time arrives, He won't delay a minute.

Guruji's words were surely prophetic. On the evening of her passing, Mildred was going about her duties in her usual practical way. Mary Crawford, who had helped and served her for so many years after Doctor's passing, was with her. Mildred stepped into an adjoining room for a moment, when she quietly called out, "Mary, I don't feel too well." By the time Mary reached Mildred's side, she had already left the body. And that, I think, is what Master was saying: "When the time arrives"—when God is ready to call you—"He won't delay a minute."

But though the body passes away, the soul that we cherish is not lost. Master said:

"Those who look only to the body will have their eyes dimmed with tears when that body must go. But those who look to the indwelling spirit will hold on to a lasting joy, because they know the soul is immortal. Death cannot touch it at all.

"Advanced devotees on earth can consciously broadcast vibratory communications to advanced devotees in the astral world. But even the ordinary man has power to waft his weightless thoughts in love toward departed dear ones. The vibrations of good thoughts are never lost, but are a quiet stimulus of joy and well-being to those beloved ones who have gone on to the astral world."

We ask Mildred to receive not only our joy in her freedom (which we should keep uppermost in our minds), but also to understand our tears of sadness at parting, because those too are expressions of love.

Such devotees of the Guru as Mildred and Doctor, and others, past, present, and future—Rajarsi Janakananda, Sri Daya Mata, and those yet to come—are an eternal blessing to this work of Self-Realization Fellowship. Souls who come to play a significant role in the ongoing mission of an avatar can never be lost to us, for they leave behind enduring monuments of spirit—not monuments of stone, which crumble with age; but a lasting legacy of inspiration and strength.

Our dear Mildred, though you have escaped our mortal sight and presence, never shall you escape our hearts and our thoughts. In the love of God and Guru, we shall never, never part.

Interior of Self-Realization Temple, San Diego, California, where for twelve years Dr. Lewis presided regularly at Sunday services

Self-Realization Fellowship Temple in San Diego, California

AT KRIYA INITIATION

(From left) Dr. Lewis, Paramahansa Yogananda, Rajarsi Janakananda, Yogacharya J. Oliver Black, and Brother Bhaktananda at *Kriya Yoga* initiation ceremony, SRF International Headquarters, during 1951 Convocation

PARAMAHANSA YOGANANDA
AND THREE MINISTERS

(From left) Brother Bhaktananda, Dr. Lloyd Kennell, Paramahansaji, and Dr. Lewis; on grounds of Self-Realization Temple, San Diego, 1947. The hilltop temple, dedicated in 1943, overlooks the distant San Diego harbor.

How to Recognize a True Master

BY DR. M. W. LEWIS

From a talk given at Self-Realization Fellowship Temple, San Diego, California

It is difficult to recognize a true master until we have learned to know the real values in life; yet there are certain fundamentals by which almost anyone can distinguish a real master from those who are merely self-appointed teachers.

Jesus spoke about this subject; in the twenty-third chapter of Matthew he talks to the people about the scribes and Pharisees who gave orders to others. But "all their work," he says, "they do for to be seen of men: they make broad their phylacteries and enlarge the borders of their garments"—indicating their indulgence of the ego consciousness—"and love the uppermost rooms at feasts, and the chief seats in the synagogues"; that is, they want to be in positions of prominence. And they want "to be called of men, *Rabbi, Rabbi.*" But Jesus cautions, "be not ye called *Rabbi,* for one is your Master, even Christ: and all ye are brethren. And call no man your father upon the earth, for one is your Father, which is in heaven. Neither be ye called masters: for one is your Master, even Christ."

Jesus thus makes it clear that all true masters speak and act from the state of Christ consciousness. We find the same idea in the Hindu scriptures; an example is the life of Jadava Krishna, who also manifested that consciousness of the universal Christ.* So if you are following a teacher, or planning to follow one, remember to ask yourself this question: Has this person lifted himself from the outward ego consciousness to real oneness with the Christ within and the omniscience of God?

When Jesus made statements such as "Verily I say unto you...my words shall not pass away," he was not speaking as the man Jesus; it

* "Christ" or "Christ Consciousness" is the projected consciousness of God immanent in all creation. In Christian scripture it is called the "only begotten son," the only pure reflection in creation of God the Father; in Hindu scripture it is called *Kutastha Chaitanya* or *Tat,* the cosmic intelligence of Spirit everywhere present in creation. It is the universal consciousness, oneness with God, manifested by Jesus, Krishna, and other great masters.

was the Christ Consciousness within him that spoke. Any true master knows whereof he speaks; and he acts with an unbiased mind and in an unprejudiced way. It is not possible to act in this way until the functions of the mind—the senses and the intellectual faculties—have been mastered, and are no longer controlled by the ego.

Very few teachers have this perfect self-control, but it is necessary in order to rightly guide other devotees; that is, to act truly from the high standpoint of Christ consciousness with only one aim: the devotee's highest good. If one feels any selfish attachment, any personal likes and dislikes, he cannot really help another in an unbiased and unprejudiced way, for he is being influenced by the whims and habits of the ego, even if unaware of it. But if one can rise above the ego consciousness and master not only the physical body but the mind and emotions as well, then he can give true help to others; for then the omniscience of God is free to speak and work through him.

When I met Paramahansa Yogananda, I was watching for this, because I had been fooled by others. But I found in all my dealings with him that he always acted without personal motive and always for my highest good. Even the first time I met him—it was in Boston on a Christmas Eve—he convinced me of this. I received so much spiritual help from him that I can never repay him; and he was obviously in a position to ask for certain things if he had wanted to. Yet all he said to me was, "Doctor, if after practicing these teachings and allowing me to discipline you, you enjoy it and find that it helps you, will you help others to follow?" "Certainly," I said, for I could see he was asking without thought of personal gain.

Not too long before his *mahasamadhi,* Paramahansaji called me on the telephone early one morning and began to reprimand me severely. When you allow a true master to discipline you, you want to be able to take it and remember that he is working to free you from bondage to the ego. But that morning he was disciplining me for something I had not done. At first, I tried to get a word in edgewise, without succeeding. Then, realizing it was greater to accept the discipline, even though undeserved, I took it gracefully. After a scolding of two or three hours, I said, "All right, sir; you win. I take the responsibility."

At that moment, when the battle with myself was over, the ego ceased to bother me. I knew I had made a spiritual step forward. Whether a man of God seems right or wrong from the viewpoint of ego consciousness, you will never lose by following his guidance. I think the Master chastised me on this occasion just to test me. Later that morning he called again and said rather sheepishly, "How are you feeling? Are you all right?" I replied, "Yes, I'm all right." Then the Master showed me his motive by saying, "No one else would have dared to talk to you like that. But I want you to gain the highest; that's why I did it."

Who else but a true master, your best friend, would do that for you? If the devotee is willing, the master can lift him from ego consciousness into awareness of God. That is why he is called a master—because he can help, but has no personal motive and expects no personal gain.

Another way in which you can recognize a true master is by the peace and bliss of the Christ Consciousness that the master exudes. This is very different from the animal magnetism some people have, which causes you to feel a certain power in their presence. I remember meeting one of the members of President Coolidge's Cabinet, in whom I felt a very definite power. But its effect is vastly different from the soul satisfaction we receive from a master. Many times we go to a master with questions, and we do not ask them because it becomes unnecessary. The soul is satisfied just by being in his presence, for we receive the benediction of the Holy Ghost* through him.

In the Bhagavad Gita,† the Lord says that "whoever shall declare the supreme secret among my devotees is one with Me; no one performs dearer service to Me than he, nor shall any other be more beloved of Me, on earth, than he." The supreme secret is not conveyed by just saying, "God is with you." It is an actual gift to you of some manifestation of Spirit. When a woman had been healed by touching the hem of Jesus' garment, he said, "Somebody hath touched me: for I perceive that virtue is gone out of me."‡ He was indicating that spiritual power had gone from him to the one who had touched him. A true master gives you a portion of the Holy Ghost, the vibration of God's power within him.

The question of personality often comes up in trying to differentiate a master from a good teacher. Masters naturally have strong

* The "Comforter" or holy vibration of *Aum*. See page 43.

† Chapter 18, verse 68.

‡ Luke 8:46.

personalities, because they are continually aware of the presence of God flowing through them. But they use that strength of personality to lift others from delusion into divine consciousness. A true master cannot help attracting people, because the power of God in him is so tremendous that nearly everyone feels it. When scientists put two masses of critical fissionable material together, an atomic reaction takes place, exerting a great force for considerable distance. If there is that much energy in apparently inert matter, how much more power is there in a master, who is consciously attuned to God! When we are with a master, that force causes a subtle elevating vibration in our spiritual and even our physical body; and just as the highly vibrating atoms in the critical mass are transmuted from matter into energy, so our material consciousness is uplifted into the presence of God by His power flowing through the master.

However, a master never possesses another person. He attracts and uplifts others, but never takes advantage of that attraction; he turns them to God for the glorification of God and the gain of the devotee, and only for that.

Masters never use their personal magnetism for material gain. They sacrifice themselves always for the devotee's spiritual benefit. If they do not, they are not true masters. During Paramahansaji's early years in America, at a time he was badly in need of money to support his organization, a man came to him and said, "Here is a check for $25,000—let me take charge of your work." The Master replied, "If you want to give me the money to use as God tells me to use it, all right. Otherwise I won't touch it." A true man of God never compromises his divine ideals.

Another quality that true masters have is love—a wonderful unconditional love that is even greater than that of our own mother and father, for parental love is circumscribed and conditional. Parents love us because they have made possible our temporal physical birth; but a master gives us spiritual birth into God's kingdom of eternity. If you are a parent and can expand your love into the impartial, all-encompassing love of God, then your entire family will be bettered. Jesus manifested this great love and compassion. He might have done many things in retaliation for that which was done to him, but he sacrificed himself always, and even on the cross he said, "Father, forgive them, for they know not what they do." He had the divine, expanded love that is one with God's omnipresent love, that extended even to those who were responsible for the destruction of his physical body.

There are many preachers of spiritual things, but few true masters of spiritual law. I had two or three wonderful teachers when I first began to search for Truth. They told me, for instance, how the great light of God is focused in the medulla center at the base of the brain, and how the medulla is like a magnifying glass concentrating that light to form the physical body. But I was unable to find anyone who could show me that light or other mysteries of the Spirit. When I met Paramahansaji, I told him about this, and he said, "Can the blind lead the blind? They both fall into the same ditch." This made a great impression on me. The Master did not give me mere theory; he *showed* me that ring of concentrated spiritual light coming in through the medulla; and he showed me other things. I saw then the difference between theory and realization. A master teaches through direct experience.

We can also recognize a true master through certain physical signs. He has complete control of his body, muscles, mind, and emotions, and remains calm under all conditions—no matter how adverse. Once I came to Paramahansaji with information about a disastrous happening. I thought he would be upset, or at least made uneasy, as I was. But he remained unmoved, exhibiting no sign of restlessness or other disturbance. I told him afterward, "Master, I wish I had your conviction that God is with me, as He is with you." He answered, "Remember, the same Father who protects me, protects you. He is our common Father." With that reply came a realization such as only a master can give. Ever since then I have felt that assurance in God.

People are always expecting a master to perform miracles, but a true master does so only when he has God's sanction. Jesus did not always perform the miracles that others expected of him. When he was captured by the servants of the chief priests and led away to be tried, he said he could summon twelve legions of angels. He had the power to save himself, for God was with him as the Christ Consciousness, but he knew it was not what his Father wanted. Earlier he had said, "O my Father, if it be possible, let this cup pass from me: nevertheless not as I will but as Thou wilt." That wonderful obedience to God's will is another sign of a true master.

In India, Paramahansaji was once called to the house of someone who was dying. The people were begging the Master to come in, saying the dying one would then recover. Finally Paramahansaji entered, and that person was healed. I was talking to the Master about this, and I said, "Sir, when you went in, you *knew* it was God's will." "Yes," he responded, "or I would never have done it." True masters act only when God says, "All right, go ahead." They know God is the sole Doer, that only by His will working through them can they accomplish anything. Every master knows this; a master is the epitome of humbleness, and desires only to do God's will.

These are a few of the ways by which you can recognize a real man of God. But if you cannot perceive any of these things through the ordinary senses or the intellect, then still the waves of the restless mind in deep meditation and your heart will tell you when you are in the presence of a true master.

Dr. Lewis *(at microphone, under umbrella at left)* and Self-Realizationists at 1951 Convocation garden party, international headquarters, Los Angeles

The Path of True Discipleship

BY DR. M. W. LEWIS

Extracts from a talk at the Self-Realization Fellowship Temple, Hollywood, California

According to the dictionary, a disciple is one who accepts and follows a teacher or doctrine. But what is a *true* disciple? There is quite a difference between ordinary discipleship and true discipleship.

I can illustrate this point by an incident that occurred when Paramahansa Yogananda was in India in 1935. While there he met a Dr. Mukherji, who was a disciple of Bhupendra Nath Sanyal, one of Lahiri Mahasaya's direct disciples. Learning that Dr. Mukherji was going to America, Paramahansaji gave him a letter for me. After Dr. Mukherji arrived, we were talking about Lahiri Mahasaya and Paramahansaji, when he asked me, "Are you a disciple of your Master?" I answered, "I think I am." "Well," he said, "someone in India asked him that, and he didn't have much to say."

So far as I knew, everything was all right between me and the Master, and although I didn't quite understand, I was not unduly disturbed. Years later, when the book *Sayings of Paramahansa Yogananda* was published in 1952, I found this passage:

"One of the disciples said to Paramahansaji, 'Master, Dr. Lewis was your first disciple in this country, wasn't he?' The Master answered, 'That's what they say.' Seeing that the questioner was a little taken aback, he added, 'I never say that people are my disciples. God is the Guru. They are His disciples.'" So in this way I received the answer to the question of true discipleship. A master, even in all his greatness, humbly recognizes that the disciples are not his, but the Heavenly Father's. So true discipleship means to follow the path that takes you back to God, the path of a true guru.

Ordinary disciples have teachers, but true disciples have a guru. There is quite a difference between a teacher and a guru. The teacher can inform you about the theory of spiritual practices, and even give you techniques whereby you can behold the great light of God. But the guru can intercede for you and take you to God.

God chooses certain spiritual channels to work through, and the beloved Master and his line of gurus is one of those channels—a great one! In the *Self-Realization Fellowship Lessons,* the Master wrote the following: "A guru, ordained by God to help individuals in response to their deep prayers, is not an ordinary teacher; but is a human vehicle whose body, speech, mind, and spirituality God uses....to guide lost souls back to His home of immortality." Now the guru may or may not be on this plane. It doesn't make a particle of difference, as you will realize if you understand what the Master has written: "A vehicle of God whose body, speech, mind, and spirituality God uses." Paramahansaji's body is no longer with us, but his *spirituality* is. That's the important point.

The Master's spirituality is a manifestation of the omniscience and unconditional love of God. That is why the Guru, even though not present in the physical body, being one with the omnipresent omniscience of God, is nevertheless with us. We should not be too much taken up with the play, the drama of life, but should seek the Reality underneath the drama, the great Light of the omniscient God. There you will find the Guru. God uses a particular being because, having omniscience, his spirituality goes beyond the physical body. The guru can therefore help the devotee while in the body and also when the body is discarded.

You can understand now what a real guru is. Our Guru has given the ways and the means whereby we can contact him through his omniscience in oneness with God, and we have nothing to do but follow the path he has laid down, the path of true discipleship. This will settle the question that may have arisen in the minds of some of you about the necessity of the physical presence of the Master.

He told me many times, "I will be nearer when I am through with the body than before." And this is indeed a fact. The light of God is the reality. "Never mind what happens to me," the Master often said. "Seek God; feel Him. That Light which you see is far greater than I am. That is God Himself." In these words the Master was breaking up the idea of a physical guru, a personality. And he was instilling in me the realization that the Sole Doer in this universe is God; His omniscience and omnipotence are everywhere. The guru has Christ Consciousness: the intelligence of God the Father manifest in all creation.

Our parents have given us physical birth, but the guru gives us the birth of spiritual consciousness. Not only this, he stays with us until we reach our home in the cosmic consciousness of God. That is the spiritual law; that is God's law, and God's grace. The words of Sri Yukteswarji,

Paramahansaji's guru, explained this beautifully, when he said to our Master, his disciple, "I shall be your friend forever, because God has asked me to bring you home." That applies to each and every one of us. God is not partial; He could not be. He is the Master of the universe; He is in each one of us. And so He has sent our beloved Master as the channel to bring us home to Him. And our Master will be with us and stay with us if we do the things he admonished us to do: regular meditation with devotion, following the path the Master has laid down. I think those words, "I shall be your friend forever," are most comforting. Did you ever have a friend such as that—a friend who has the power to stick by you through incarnations, until he can take you back to your home of omnipresence, oneness with God?

The path of true discipleship leads directly to God. It is not a winding, crooked way. It is not the way of the world. It is the straight way to God. The Bible tells us this in St. John 1:23: "I am the voice of one crying in the wilderness. Make straight the way of the Lord, as said the prophet Isaiah."

Who knows the straight way to God? Not many teachers you may have known. But the guru knows the straight way, because his consciousness is one with the omniscience of God, and he can take you in the shortest possible time back to the Home whence you came, if you follow him with devotion and the same love that he gives to you.

What is the "voice" of that "straight way"? It is the Intelligent Cosmic Vibration, the sound of *Aum,* the great Amen. In that voice God speaks to those who are in tune. If you can merge your consciousness in that Holy Vibration, you become one with the omniscience of God in that vibration. This the guru teaches us how to do. In St. John 1:1 we read: "In the beginning was the Word, and the Word was with God, and the Word was God." And so the techniques that the Master has brought to us take us straight into the presence of God within us, the Holy Vibration. Merge in that and you are following the path of true discipleship; you are a disciple of God, because He is that Holy Vibration. But if you learn only theory and words, and listen to those who have not attuned themselves to the omniscience of God, how can you expect to merge your consciousness into His presence? It's impossible. It is when you follow the instructions of a true guru that you are on the straight way back to your home in God.

God is all. As the great creative *Aum* or Amen, He is vibrating universe upon universe, world upon world, human being upon human being. Merge in Him. The Master said, "Seek God alone." He said of himself and the tremendous responsibilities of his organizational work throughout the world, which he carried single-handedly, "If I had not had that realization of God alone, I would not have been able to keep my head above the delusive troubles of organization." When you realize God alone, nothing—nothing—can put you down. Nothing can disturb you.

The path of true discipleship under the guru will lead unfailingly to God-consciousness. When we achieve contact with God as the Holy Vibration, through the techniques of Self-Realization Fellowship, we will have communion with God—we will *know* Him. And in that consciousness, in the light and love of the One Guru, God, we will know him whom God has sent—His channel, our beloved guru, Paramahansa Yogananda.

Dr. Lewis with children of the Self-Realization Fellowship Sunday School, San Diego, California, after dedication services for their new meeting-place, March 18, 1956

Positive Results of Meditation

By Dr. M. W. Lewis

What positive results can we expect from meditation? It seems to me that one of the greatest blessings is a steadily increasing peace, poise, and calmness. This is especially noticeable when we give meditation preference over our other activities, and practice it with regularity, fullest attention, and devotion. To perform right actions in our lives—that is, to act according to the Divine Will—it is of paramount importance that we attain the great calmness that comes only from meditation, for it is only in calmness that the silent, never-failing guidance of the soul, whispered through intuition, can be heard.

We find also that pain and trouble cease to cause us so much annoyance. Not that pain and trouble necessarily leave us! but through meditation we realize our real selves as beyond these things, and therefore unaffected by them. The underlying principle of this is that the desires of the heart can be permanently and completely satisfied only by turning our attention inward toward the soul, the source of all happiness—for the soul is Bliss Itself. When our desires for outward things are not fulfilled, we experience pain and sorrow because of that unfulfillment. But when we realize the soul, we find we have everything. We have the source of all contentment, and are therefore unaffected by the fulfillment or unfulfillment of our desires.

Meditation takes us to the soul. Or we might say, meditation brings about an attunement of body and mind that is favorable to soul expression. The soul tries constantly to express itself; but because our physical and mental instruments are not always functioning in consonance with the soul's nature, its divine qualities are unable to blossom forth to the fullest extent.

Meditation brings us ever so much closer to Spirit than intellectual learning can. In fact, it seems strange that men of great intellect, men with keen minds, sometimes cannot understand, or do not have the inclination to know, matters pertaining to the Spirit. Why? Because to realize the soul we have to feel and know through intuition; which is pure knowing, without the intervention of the intellect or sensory impressions. Thus when perception comes through intuition, we are above the mind and intellect. This is why we have to try so hard to still the waves of the intellectually and sensorially agitated mind. When we have done this, intuition can act, as it is always trying to do. If we hold a vessel of water in our hand, and keep the water still, we can see clearly in it the image of the sun shining above. But if we move the vessel and disturb the water, the sun image becomes distorted. By this we can understand why the intellectual man who does not know how to still the waves of the mind and rise above its limited capabilities cannot comprehend things of the Spirit.

But do not think that we should not have keen minds and intellects. In fact, don't worry about it. Lift the consciousness to Spirit first, and then the power of Spirit, working through unhampered intuition, will percolate through the lower mental processes, and the mind and intellect will be sharpened a thousandfold. Those who meditate deeply understand many things that purely intellectual men are unable to comprehend.

Therefore, let us meditate well. Be neither misled by the glamor of matter nor sidetracked by lesser manifestations of Spirit. Dive deep into the ocean of Spirit and find the real jewels of realization.

Meditation will adjust all conditions of ignorance or imperfection, for it takes our consciousness to the Fountainhead—the all-knowing Spirit, our common Father, the Creator and Sustainer of us all.

Dr. Lewis greets Brother Nityananda in Encinitas. The Lewises had just returned, on November 27, 1956, from a visit to Boston.

The Cure of Sorrow

BY DR. M. W. LEWIS

Sunday service, Self-Realization Fellowship Temple, San Diego, California

There is a Reality behind outward consciousness that we must and can know. When we know this Reality, then sorrow will be secondary.

A few lines of verse might be appropriate here: "It is easy enough to sing and shout / When life goes along like a song. / But the man worthwhile is the man with a smile / When everything goes dead wrong." Now the "dead wrong" consciousness is not necessary. What *is* necessary is a positive inner awareness of the Eternal Verity behind our outward consciousness of alternating joy and sorrow, pleasure and pain. It is because our minds are tied to outward perceptions of change that a dead wrong situation comes about. But when we are inwardly conscious of God's great light and love, nothing can be dead wrong.

You know about the optimist who fell ten stories, shouting as he passed each window, "All right—so far!" And you know some really super-optimistic people who say there's nothing so bad that it couldn't be worse. Isn't that a little hypocritical? Unless you know the Reality behind this drama of life, which seems so real to us,* you cannot truly say that. When you realize the Reality, it's all right to say such things, because you've got something that fortifies you against all outward conditions of uncertainty, change, and chance in this delusive dream-consciousness of God.† So let us realize that the cure for sorrow, in a few words, is to know

* "Just as cinematic images appear to be real but are only combinations of light and shade, so is the universal variety a delusive seeming....Temporarily true to man's five sense perceptions, the transitory scenes are cast on the screen of human consciousness by the infinite creative beam.

"A cinema audience may look up and see that all screen images are appearing through the instrumentality of one imageless beam of light. The colorful universal drama is similarly issuing from the single white light of a Cosmic Source. With inconceivable ingenuity God is staging 'super-colossal' entertainment for His children, making them actors as well as audience in His planetary theater."—Paramahansa Yogananda in *Autobiography of a Yogi.*

† "A dreamer is not cognizant of the hallucinatory fabric of a dream until he awakens. Similarly, man does not understand the delusory nature of the cosmic dream of creation until he awakens in God."—*Sayings of Paramahansa Yogananda.*

that Consciousness which does not change, which is stable. Having That, we have everything.

Analyze the Sources of Sorrow

There are three main causes of sorrow. First is identification with the outer experiences of our consciousness— "this is mine," "my finger hurts," "my house burned down." There can be no peace in that, and there will be sorrow. The second cause is the working of the law of karma. The law being fulfilled—as it surely will be—produces sorrow. And finally, the third cause of sorrow is ignorance. Ignorance is the greatest obstacle, because it prevents us from knowing that we are really children of God, rays of the eternal flame of Spirit.

I was reading in Sri Yukteswarji's *The Holy Science* a few words that explain, far better than I can, the cause of sorrow: "So long, however, as man identifies himself with his material body and fails to find repose in his true Self, he feels his wants according as his heart's desires remain unsatisfied." How can they be satisfied in outward consciousness? They cannot be. Then he goes on to say that so long as man lives in this consciousness, he has to suffer "all the troubles of life and death, not only in the present but in the future as well." Thus, identification with outward consciousness is one of the main causes of sorrow. Outward or worldly consciousness had a beginning, therefore it must have an ending; and, being unstable, all things connected with that consciousness, especially when it has been mistaken for reality, must cause sorrow.

Be Fixed in the Stable Consciousness of God

We have said that the first cause of sorrow is identification with outward or changing consciousness. Now let me give you one or two illustrations. For instance, we see loved ones, friends, families, opportunities, and possessions slip away. What is the result? Sorrow. And perhaps when you're young and full of pep and ambition, you say, "I'm going to lay away something for a rainy day; I'm going to do this and I'm going to do that, and when I get along a little bit I'm going to sit down and take it easy." But sometimes those plans are altered and that provision for a rainy day doesn't come through. Why? Because we're not acting in the right consciousness of God and His great love and bliss; we are acting in the changing consciousness of worldly existence. That's why it doesn't always work out. What is the result? Sorrow.

Another illustration comes to mind. We plan great things for our children, but sometimes they disappoint us. We are disappointed because we regard our children with possessiveness and attachment. We do not think of them as children of God, given to us to take care of for just a little while. We have only one obligation—to do the best we can for our children, and if we do it completely and thoroughly there will be no sorrow. Do the best you can as God shows you. If you act with that spirit and that consciousness, there will be no grief, no matter what the child does, because you know you've done your best.

Thus sorrow is the product of identification with outward, changing, transient consciousness—with all its paradoxes and its uncertainties and its injustices. But if we are fixed in that stable consciousness which is our true self—that presence of God within us that does not change—then we can view this ever-changing drama of life without being affected, because God is with us. And "if God be for us, who can be against us?"* How can we be sorrowful when we are one with God, the Master of the universe? That's what we must strive for; that is the cure for sorrow.

You Can Escape From Karmic Sufferings

Now, going on to the operation of the law of karma: It is the working of this law that produces in us latent tendencies and impulses, which in turn place us in the three situations I have just described to you. The law of cause and effect works in such a way that because of our previous actions in other lives, and our actions in this life, we are placed in a situation whereby we have attachments—for children, for money, for position. If this is your situation, never mind, you're in it; you're in it because the law of karma has put you there. That doesn't mean you've got to stay there. But while the law of karma is working out, it is a cause of sorrow. It is because of the tendencies you have, the latent impulses, that you are placed in a particular situation wherein your action brings sorrow. You cannot help acting as you do because the law of karma has to be fulfilled. But you can stop it right from this moment on, if you will.

For instance, in the illustration of planning for a rainy day, what is the trouble? The law of karma has made you put too much emphasis and dependence on material things rather than on the inner gifts of God. Also, in the illustration of our attitude toward our children, instead

*Romans 8:31.

of having a broad view of them as children of God, we have taken the narrow view of them as *our* children. As a result, we suffer. If the child is wayward, you may say, "Why did it have to be *my* child?" If because of his actions the child has to be put away from society, you say, "Why did it happen to *me*?" It happened to you because the law of karma worked and demanded, on account of your child's karma and your karma, that you come together and that this thing happen. So if you realize the true cause, then even with all your sadness, no matter how trying and nerve-wracking and heartbreaking the condition is, you can realize the one consciousness of God and escape from suffering.

If you realize the light of God, the darkness of sorrow cannot stay, because God's light is supreme. Get hold of God—that's the only way out. Having Him, you will be saved from future trouble. The desires arising from the attachment of outward consciousness produce wants within us, and when we have wants, we have sorrow. We must go beyond that and seek the Reality. Having Him, wants will not bother us, as we will have sufficiency in the fullness of God within.

Ignorance Prevents Us From Knowing Our Divine Nature

Now, the last and greatest cause of sorrow is ignorance. Why? Because it prevents us from realizing our true nature; from understanding that we are not this body, that this outward consciousness and world is not the reality, is not the true picture. Ignorance prevents us from knowing that we are really children of God; templed in each one of us is a ray of the one eternal Spirit. Consider your soul, and you will realize that you have not done your best to make this vehicle a temple of God. No doubt the greatest sorrow is to realize at the end of the trail, when the drama of life is over, that you have not given your best. We have the channel of the beloved Guru, Paramahansa Yogananda, who has sacrificed so much for us that if only we would follow his teachings and spiritual techniques, we could easily reach that awareness of God's presence wherein sorrow is permanently removed. Think how miserable you will feel when you realize you have not done your best to follow the channel God has sent. That realization will produce for you the greatest sorrow imaginable. You must do something about it.

Never forget that the Master's consciousness is always dynamically vibrating in the divine ether. He is waiting for all who will to contact it and be forever free from sorrow in the blissful consciousness of the Heavenly Father, even as the Guru is one with the consciousness of that common Father of you, of me, of Jesus, of all saints. It is not a dead thing—it is dynamic right this minute. If you make up your mind to start now to contact God, you can be rid of sorrow.

For the moment you set your heart to understand, and then begin to discipline yourself, begin to merge in that consciousness of God within, then God will come, if you mean business with Him. Get busy and follow the channel He has sent, because the Master's love and consciousness are vibrating in the divine eternal, and always will be. The great presence of God is in each and every one of us, that great eternal light of God. It is yours if you will have it. Make the effort.

Dwell in the Consciousness of God

So the cure of sorrow is to be in that consciousness where you'll be permanently free from it. Isn't that true? And to be in the consciousness of God within is the first and greatest commandment. That is why Jesus said, "Thou shalt love the Lord thy God with all thy heart, and with all thy soul, and with all thy mind, and with all thy strength."* It is not only the greatest commandment, it is your greatest necessity; because you will not permanently be free from sorrow until you contact His presence, until you merge in it. It's not hard, because God sent the channel of the Master, and through his efforts and sacrifices he has made it quite easy; but we're so lazy and so indifferent, we do not realize it. We want to do it, but we don't have the "get up and do" spirit to resolve that from this moment on, the greatest necessity of life is to be one with God. Let us realize that and make the effort. The delusion is so great. Divine Mother says, "Oh, I'll give you this, I'll give you that, I'll give you everything." And She almost convinces us. But we will never have any peace with outward things, only with the presence of Divine Mother Herself. That's what we must have, not Her gifts.

And so in conclusion I would like to corroborate these things I have said by reading a few passages from the scriptures. I want you to listen carefully. These are eternal truths. First, from the Bhagavad Gita:

"Unattracted to the sensory world, the yogi experiences the ever new joy of Being. His soul engaged in the union with Spirit"—which is the experience of Self-realization—"he attains indestructible bliss."† Can there be any sorrow there? No. "Because...sense pleasures spring from outward contacts"—that is, the objects perceived through the outward

* Mark 12:30. † Bhagavad Gita V:21.

sense consciousness—"and have beginning and end...they lead only to misery. No sage seeks happiness from them"*—for the wise see beyond that. Don't let Divine Mother fool you. She's going to try to see if you really want Her. So do not seek comfort and satisfaction through the contacts of outward consciousness. Go thou into the Fountainhead, the Divine Mother Herself.

Finally, from the Bible; you have heard it many times, but listen again. "I am the door: by me if any man enter in, he shall be saved"—that is, there can be no sorrow in God-consciousness. You shall be saved not only from evil but from all sorrow—"he shall be saved, and shall go in and out, and find pasture."† Now, Self-Realization Fellowship gives you the methods and the techniques whereby you can enter the door into the presence of God within, into that great eternal Light we read of in St. John: "That was the true light, which lighteth every man that cometh into the world."‡ Every one of us has that eternal flame within, and every one of us can see it, if we know the way to look and to pass through the door, the spiritual eye at the point between the eyebrows. There you will feel the light of God. Nothing can touch it for taking away sorrow. Know that light, be one with it.

There Is No Peace Like the Presence of God

Again in St. John, we read, "Peace I leave with you, my peace I give unto you."§ There is no peace like the presence of God. It is not the worldly peace. The peace that Jesus expressed when Christ Consciousness was flowing through him, that is what he left with his disciples; and that is what will be left with everyone who follows and becomes one with and merges in that Christ Consciousness. The Master is in that, he has that consciousness; it is waiting for us. "Peace I leave with you, my peace I give unto you. Not as the world giveth, give I unto you."** And again in St. John we read, "In the world ye shall have tribulation."†† In outward consciousness you cannot escape it. Don't expect to. There will be sorrow and trouble; but Jesus goes on to say, "Be of good cheer, I have overcome the world."‡‡ That is, "I have overcome worldly consciousness." Jesus had to overcome, each and every one of us can overcome, and that is the key to the cure of sorrow. Overcome worldly consciousness. In the bliss of God there can be no sorrow. In that bliss of God you can believe; that is the Reality.

* Bhagavad Gita V:22. † John 10:9. ‡ John 1:9. § John 14:27.
** Ibid. †† John 16:33. ‡‡ Ibid.

About Paramahansa Yogananda

"The ideal of love for God and service to humanity found full expression in the life of Paramahansa Yogananda.... Though the major part of his life was spent outside India, still he takes his place among our great saints. His work continues to grow and shine ever more brightly, drawing people everywhere on the path of the pilgrimage of the Spirit."

In these words, the Government of India paid tribute to the founder of Self-Realization Fellowship/Yogoda Satsanga Society of India, upon issuing a commemorative stamp in his honor on March 7, 1977, the twenty-fifth anniversary of his passing.

Paramahansa Yogananda began his life's work in India in 1917 with the founding of a "how-to-live" school for boys, where modern educational methods were combined with yoga training and instruction in spiritual ideals. In 1920 he was invited to Boston as India's representative to an International Congress of Religious Liberals. Subsequent lectures in Boston, New York, and Philadelphia were enthusiastically received, and in 1924 he embarked on a cross-continental speaking tour.

For the next decade Paramahansaji traveled extensively, giving lectures and classes in which he instructed thousands of men and women in the yoga science of meditation and balanced spiritual living. In 1925 he established the Self-Realization Fellowship International Headquarters in Los Angeles, and from there the spiritual and humanitarian work he began continues under the direction of Brother Chidananda, president of Self-Realization Fellowship/Yogoda Satsanga Society of India. In addition to publishing Paramahansa Yogananda's writings, lectures, and informal talks (including a comprehensive series of lessons on the science of *Kriya Yoga* meditation), the society oversees Self-Realization Fellowship temples, retreats, and meditation centers around the world; monastic training programs; and a Worldwide Prayer Circle, which serves as a channel to help bring healing to those in need and greater peace and harmony among all nations.

Quincy Howe, Jr., Ph.D., Professor of Ancient Languages, Scripps College, wrote: "Paramahansa Yogananda brought to the West not only India's perennial promise of God-realization, but also a practical method by which spiritual aspirants from all walks of life may progress rapidly toward that goal. Originally appreciated in the West only on the most lofty and abstract level, the spiritual legacy of India is now accessible as practice and experience to all who aspire to know God, not in the beyond, but in the here and now....Yogananda has placed within the reach of all the most exalted methods of contemplation."

The life and teachings of Paramahansa Yogananda are described in his *Autobiography of a Yogi,* which has become a classic in its field since its publication in 1946 and is now used as a text and reference work in colleges and universities throughout the world. An award-winning documentary film about Paramahansa Yogananda's life and work, *Awake: The Life of Yogananda,* was released in October 2014.

Autobiography of a Yogi

"A rare account."—*The New York Times*

"A fascinating and clearly annotated study."—*Newsweek*

"There has been nothing before, written in English or in any other European language, like this presentation of Yoga."—*Columbia University Press*

"These pages reveal, with incomparable strength and clarity, a fascinating life, a personality of such unheard-of greatness, that from beginning to end the reader is left breathless. We must credit this book with the power to bring about a spiritual revolution."—*Schleswig-Holsteinische Tagespost,* Germany

AIMS AND IDEALS
of
Self-Realization Fellowship

As set forth by Paramahansa Yogananda, Founder

Brother Chidananda, President

To disseminate among the nations a knowledge of definite scientific techniques for attaining direct personal experience of God.

To teach that the purpose of life is the evolution, through self-effort, of man's limited mortal consciousness into God Consciousness; and to this end to establish Self-Realization Fellowship temples for God-communion throughout the world, and to encourage the establishment of individual temples of God in the homes and in the hearts of men.

To reveal the complete harmony and basic oneness of original Christianity as taught by Jesus Christ and original Yoga as taught by Bhagavan Krishna; and to show that these principles of truth are the common scientific foundation of all true religions.

To point out the one divine highway to which all paths of true religious beliefs eventually lead: the highway of daily, scientific, devotional meditation on God.

To liberate man from his threefold suffering: physical disease, mental inharmonies, and spiritual ignorance.

To encourage "plain living and high thinking"; and to spread a spirit of brotherhood among all peoples by teaching the eternal basis of their unity: kinship with God.

To demonstrate the superiority of mind over body, of soul over mind.

To overcome evil by good, sorrow by joy, cruelty by kindness, ignorance by wisdom.

To unite science and religion through realization of the unity of their underlying principles.

To advocate cultural and spiritual understanding between East and West, and the exchange of their finest distinctive features.

To serve mankind as one's larger Self.

ADDITIONAL RESOURCES ON THE KRIYA YOGA TEACHINGS OF PARAMAHANSA YOGANANDA

Self-Realization Fellowship is dedicated to freely assisting seekers worldwide. For information regarding our annual series of public lectures and classes, meditation and inspirational services at our temples and centers around the world, a schedule of retreats, and other activities, we invite you to visit our website or our International Headquarters:

www.yogananda.org

Self-Realization Fellowship
3880 San Rafael Avenue
Los Angeles, CA 90065
(323) 225-2471

SELF-REALIZATION FELLOWSHIP LESSONS

Personal guidance and instruction from Paramahansa Yogananda on the techniques of yoga meditation and principles of spiritual living

If you feel drawn to the spiritual teachings of Paramahansa Yogananda, we invite you to enroll in the *Self-Realization Fellowship Lessons.*

Paramahansa Yogananda originated this home-study series to provide sincere seekers the opportunity to learn and practice the ancient yoga meditation techniques that he brought to the West—including the science of *Kriya Yoga.* The *Lessons* also present his practical guidance for attaining balanced physical, mental, and spiritual well-being.

The *Self-Realization Fellowship Lessons* are available at a nominal fee (to cover printing and postage costs). All students are freely given personal guidance in their practice by Self-Realization Fellowship monks and nuns.

For more information...

The scientific techniques of meditation taught by Paramahansa Yogananda, including *Kriya Yoga*—as well as his guidance on all aspects of balanced spiritual living—are taught in the *Self-Realization Fellowship Lessons.* Please visit www.srflessons.org to request a comprehensive complimentary information packet about the *Lessons,* which includes:

- *"An Overview of the Self-Realization Fellowship Lessons: Information About Paramahansa Yogananda's Home-Study Series"*
- *"Highest Achievements Through Self-Realization," by Paramahansa Yogananda—a thorough introduction to the teachings presented in the SRF Lessons*

Books by Paramahansa Yogananda

Available at bookstores or online at www.srfbooks.org

Autobiography of a Yogi

Autobiography of a Yogi (*Audiobook, read by Sir Ben Kingsley*)

God Talks With Arjuna: The Bhagavad Gita—
A New Translation and Commentary

The Second Coming of Christ: The Resurrection of the Christ Within You—A Revelatory Commentary on the Original Teachings of Jesus

The Collected Talks and Essays
Volume I: Man's Eternal Quest
Volume II: The Divine Romance
Volume III: Journey to Self-realization

Wine of the Mystic: The Rubaiyat of Omar Khayyam—
A Spiritual Interpretation

The Science of Religion

Whispers from Eternity

Songs of the Soul

Sayings of Paramahansa Yogananda

Scientific Healing Affirmations

Where There Is Light: Insight and Inspiration for Meeting Life's Challenges

In the Sanctuary of the Soul: A Guide to Effective Prayer

Inner Peace: How to Be Calmly Active and Actively Calm

How You Can Talk With God

Metaphysical Meditations

The Law of Success

Cosmic Chants

DVD Video

Awake: The Life of Yogananda
A film by CounterPoint Films

A complete catalog of books and audio/video recordings—including rare archival recordings of Paramahansa Yogananda—is available on request or online at www.srfbooks.org.

SELF-REALIZATION FELLOWSHIP
3880 San Rafael Avenue • Los Angeles, CA 90065-3219
TEL (323) 225-2471 • FAX (323) 225-5088
www.yogananda.org